COMMON CORE MATHEMATICS

NEW YORK EDITION

Grade 2, Module 1: Sums and Differences to 20

COMMON CORE

JOSSEY-BASS
A Wiley Imprint
www.josseybass.com

Published by Jossey-Bass
A Wiley Brand
One Montgomery Street, Suite 1200, San Francisco, CA 94104-4594—www.josseybass.com

ISBN 978-1-118-79293-3

Printed in the United States of America
FIRST EDITION
PB Printing   10 9 8 7 6 5 4 3 2 1

WELCOME

Dear Teacher,

Thank you for your interest in Common Core's curriculum in mathematics. Common Core is a non-profit organization based in Washington, DC dedicated to helping K-12 public schoolteachers use the power of high-quality content to improve instruction.[1] We are led by a board of master teachers, scholars, and current and former school, district, and state education leaders. Common Core has responded to the Common Core State Standards' (CCSS) call for "content-rich curriculum"[2] by creating new, CCSS-based curriculum materials in mathematics, English Language Arts, history, and (soon) the arts. All of our materials are written by teachers who are among the nation's foremost experts on the new standards.

In 2012 Common Core won three contracts from the New York State Education Department to create a PreKindergarten–12th grade mathematics curriculum for the teachers of that state, and to conduct associated professional development. The book you hold contains a portion of that work. In order to respond to demand in New York and elsewhere, modules of the curriculum will continue to be published, on a rolling basis, as they are completed. This curriculum is based on New York's version of the CCSS (the CCLS, or Common Core Learning Standards). Common Core will be releasing an enhanced version of the curriculum this summer on our website, commoncore.org. That version also will be published by Jossey-Bass, a Wiley imprint.

Common Core's curriculum materials are not merely aligned to the new standards, they take the CCSS as their very foundation. Our work in math takes its shape from the expectations embedded in the new standards—including the instructional shifts and mathematical progressions, and the new expectations for student fluency, deep conceptual understanding, and application to real-life context. Similarly, our ELA and history curricula are deeply informed by the CCSS's new emphasis on close reading, increased use of informational text, and evidence-based writing.

Our curriculum is distinguished not only by its adherence to the CCSS. The math curriculum is based on a theory of teaching math that is proven to work. That theory posits that mathematical knowledge is most coherently and

---

1. Despite the coincidence of name, Common Core and the Common Core State Standards are not affiliated. Common Core was established in 2007, prior to the start of the Common Core State Standards Initiative, which was led by the National Governors Association and the Council for Chief State School Officers.
2. *Common Core State Standards for English Language Arts & Literacy in History/Social Studies, Science, and Technical Subjects* (Washington, DC: Common Core State Standards Initiative), 6.

effectively conveyed when it is taught in a sequence that follows the "story" of mathematics itself. This is why we call the elementary portion of this curriculum "The Story of Units," to be followed by "The Story of Ratios" in middle school, and "The Story of Functions" in high school. Mathematical concepts flow logically, from one to the next, in this curriculum. The sequencing has been joined with methods of instruction that have been proven to work, in this nation and abroad. These methods drive student understanding beyond process, to deep mastery of mathematical concepts. The goal of the curriculum is to produce students who are not merely literate, but fluent, in mathematics.

It is important to note that, as extensive as these curriculum materials are, they are not meant to be prescriptive. Rather, they are intended to provide a basis for teachers to hone their own craft through study, collaboration, training, and the application of their own expertise as professionals. At Common Core we believe deeply in the ability of teachers and in their central and irreplaceable role in shaping the classroom experience. We strive only to support and facilitate their important work.

The teachers and scholars who wrote these materials are listed beginning on the next page. Their deep knowledge of mathematics, of the CCSS, and of what works in classrooms defined this work in every respect. I would like to thank Louisiana State University professor of mathematics Scott Baldridge for the intellectual leadership he provides to this project. Teacher, trainer, and writer Robin Ramos is the most inspired math educator I've ever encountered. It is Robin and Scott's aspirations for what mathematics education in America *should* look like that is spelled out in these pages.

Finally, this work owes a debt to project director Nell McAnelly that is so deep I'm confident it never can be repaid. Nell, who leads LSU's Gordon A. Cain Center for STEM Literacy, oversees all aspects of our work for NYSED. She has spent days, nights, weekends, and many cancelled vacations toiling in her efforts to make it possible for this talented group of teacher-writers to produce their best work against impossible deadlines. I'm confident that in the years to come Scott, Robin, and Nell will be among those who will deserve to be credited with putting math instruction in our nation back on track.

Thank you for taking an interest in our work. Please join us at www.commoncore.org.

Lynne Munson
President and Executive Director
Common Core
Washington, DC
June 20, 2013

Common Core's K-5 Math Staff

Scott Baldridge, Lead Mathematician and Writer
Robin Ramos, Lead Writer, PreKindergarten-5
Jill Diniz, Lead Writer, 6-12
Ben McCarty, Mathematician

Nell McAnelly, Project Director
Tiah Alphonso, Associate Director
Jennifer Loftin, Associate Director
Catriona Anderson, Curriculum Manager,
    PreKindergarten-5

Sherri Adler, PreKindergarten
Debbie Andorka-Aceves, PreKindergarten

Kate McGill Austin, Kindergarten
Nancy Diorio, Kindergarten
Lacy Endo-Peery, Kindergarten
Melanie Gutierrez, Kindergarten
Nuhad Jamal, Kindergarten
Cecilia Rudzitis, Kindergarten
Shelly Snow, Kindergarten

Beth Barnes, First Grade
Lily Cavanaugh, First Grade
Ana Estela, First Grade
Kelley Isinger, First Grade
Kelly Spinks, First Grade
Marianne Strayton, First Grade
Hae Jung Yang, First Grade

Wendy Keehfus-Jones, Second Grade
Susan Midlarsky, Second Grade
Jenny Petrosino, Second Grade
Colleen Sheeron, Second Grade
Nancy Sommer, Second Grade
Lisa Watts-Lawton, Second Grade
MaryJo Wieland, Second Grade
Jessa Woods, Second Grade

Eric Angel, Third Grade
Greg Gorman, Third Grade
Susan Lee, Third Grade
Cristina Metcalf, Third Grade
Ann Rose Santoro, Third Grade
Kevin Tougher, Third Grade
Victoria Peacock, Third Grade
Saffron VanGalder, Third Grade

Katrina Abdussalaam, Fourth Grade
Kelly Alsup, Fourth Grade
Patti Dieck, Fourth Grade
Mary Jones, Fourth Grade
Soojin Lu, Fourth Grade
Tricia Salerno, Fourth Grade
Gail Smith, Fourth Grade
Eric Welch, Fourth Grade
Sam Wertheim, Fourth Grade
Erin Wheeler, Fourth Grade

Leslie Arceneaux, Fifth Grade
Adam Baker, Fifth Grade
Janice Fan, Fifth Grade
Peggy Golden, Fifth Grade
Halle Kananak, Fifth Grade
Shauntina Kerrison, Fifth Grade
Pat Mohr, Fifth Grade
Chris Sarlo, Fifth Grade

Additional Writers

Bill Davidson, Fluency Specialist
Robin Hecht, UDL Specialist
Simon Pfeil, Mathematician

Document Management Team

Tam Le, Document Manager
Jennifer Merchan, Copy Editor

Table of Contents

GRADE 2 • MODULE 1

Sums and Differences to 20

Grade 2 • Module 1

Sums and Differences to 20

OVERVIEW

Module 1 sets the foundation for students to master the sums and differences to 20 **(2.OA.2)** and to subsequently apply these skills to fluently add one-digit to two-digit numbers at least through 100 using place value understandings, properties of operations and the relationship between addition and subtraction **(2.NBT.5)**. In Grade 1, students worked extensively with numbers to 10 and they developed Level 2 and Level 3 mental strategies to add and subtract within 20 **(1.OA.1)** and 100 **(1.NBT.4-6)**.

Level 2: Count on   Level 3: Decompose an addend to compose ten

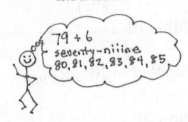   

For example, to solve 12 + 3 students might make an equivalent but easier problem by decomposing 12 as 10 + 2 and composing 2 with 3 to make 5. Students can use this knowledge to solve related problems such as 92 + 3. They also apply their skill using smaller numbers to subtract problems with larger numbers: 12 − 8 = 10 − 8 + 2 = 2 + 2, just as 72 − 8 = 70 − 8 + 2 = 62 + 2.

$$12 + 3$$
$$12 + 3 = 10 + 2 + 3 = 10 + 5$$

$$12 - 8$$
$$12 - 8 = 10 - 8 + 2 = 2 + 2$$

$$92 + 3$$
$$92 + 3 = 90 + 2 + 3 = 90 + 5$$

$$72 - 8$$
$$72 - 8 = 70 - 8 + 2 = 62 + 2$$

Daily fluency activities provide sustained practice to help students attain fluency within 20. This fluency is essential to the work of later modules and future grade levels, where students must fluently recompose place value units to work adeptly with the four operations. Activities such as Say Ten counting and Take from 10, and the use of ten-frame cards and Hide Zero cards, solidify student fluency. Because the amount of practice required by each student to achieve mastery will vary, a motivating, differentiated fluency program needs to be established in these first weeks to set the tone for the rest of the year.

Throughout the module, students will represent and solve one-step word problems through the daily Application Problem **(2.OA.1)**. Application problems can precede a lesson to act as the lead-in to a concept, allowing students to discover through problem-solving the logic and usefulness of a strategy before that strategy is reviewed. Or, they can follow the concept development so that students connect and apply their learning to real-world situations. This latter structure can also serve as a bridge between teacher-directed work and students solving problems independently on activity worksheets and at home. In either case, problem-solving begins as a guided activity, with the goal being to move students to independent problem-solving, wherein they reason through the relationships of the problem and choose an appropriate strategy to solve. In Module 1, application problems follow concept development.

Topic A reactivates students' Kindergarten and Grade 1 learning, as they practice prerequisite skills for Level 3 decomposition and composition methods: partners to 10 and decompositions for all numbers within 10^1. Students move briskly from concrete to pictorial to abstract as they remember their "make ten" facts. They use ten-frame cards to visualize 10, and they write the number bonds of 10 from memory. They use those facts to see relationships in larger numbers (e.g., 28 needs how many to make 30.) The number bond is also used to represent related facts within 10.

Topic B also moves from concrete to pictorial to abstract, as students use decomposing strategies to add and subtract within 20. By the end of Grade 1, Module 2, students learned to form ten as a unit. Hence, the phrase *make ten* now transitions to *make a ten*. Students use the ten-structure to reason about making a ten to add to the teens, and they use this pattern and math drawings to solve related problem sets (e.g., 9 + 4, 9 + 5, 9 + 6). Students reason about the relationship between problems such as 19 + 5 and 20 + 4 to 9 + 5 and 10 + 4. They use place value understanding to add and subtract within 20 by adding to and subtracting from the ones. The topic ends with a lesson in which students subtract from 10. The goal in making a 10 and taking from 10 is for students to master mental math.

$$13 + 2 = 15$$
$$\overset{\displaystyle /\,\backslash}{10 \quad 3}$$

$$3+2=5$$
$$13+2=15$$

$$15 - 3 = 12$$
$$\overset{\displaystyle /\,\backslash}{10 \quad 5}$$

$$5-3=2$$
$$15-3=12$$

$$14 - 8 = 6$$
$$\overset{\displaystyle /\,\backslash}{10 \quad 4}$$

$$10-8=2$$
$$4+2=6$$
$$14-8=6$$

Add and subtract ones

Take from 10

Topic C calls on students to review strategies to add and subtract within 100 (**1.NBT.4–6**) to set the foundation for Grade 2's work towards mastery of fluency with the same set of problems (**2.NBT.5**). They use basic facts and place value understanding to add and subtract within multiples of 10 without crossing the multiple (e.g., 7 − 5 = 2, so 47 - 5 = 42.) This segues into the use of basic facts and properties of addition to cross multiples of 10 (e.g., 26 + 9 = 20 + 6 + 4 + 5). In the final lesson, students decompose to make a ten, and then to subtract from numbers that have both tens and ones.

$$87 + 5 = 92$$
$$\overset{\displaystyle /\,\backslash \;\; /\,\backslash}{80 \;\; 7 \;\; 3 \;\; 2}$$

$$80 + 10 + 2 = 92$$

Add basic facts to cross multiples of ten

$$91 - 5 = 86$$
$$\overset{\displaystyle /\,\backslash}{81 \quad 10}$$

$$10-5=5$$
$$81 +5 = 86$$

Decompose and subtract from the 10

---

^{1} K.OA.4 and K.OA.3

| Module 1: | Sums and Differences to 20 |
| Date: | 6/25/13 |

iii

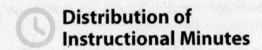

Distribution of Instructional Minutes

This diagram represents a suggested distribution of instructional minutes based on the emphasis of particular lesson components in different lessons throughout the module.

- ■ Fluency Practice
- ■ Concept Development
- ■ Application Problems
- ■ Student Debrief

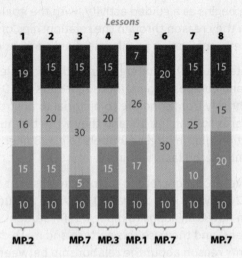

MP = Mathematical Practice

Focus Grade Level Standards

Represent and solve problems involving addition and subtraction.[2]

2.OA.1   Use addition and subtraction within 100 to solve one- and two-step word problems involving situations of adding to, taking from, putting together, taking apart, and comparing, with unknowns in all positions, e.g., by using drawings and equations with a symbol for the unknown number to represent the problem. (See Glossary, Table 1.)

Add and subtract within 20.[3]

2.OA.2   Fluently add and subtract within 20 using mental strategies. (See standard 1.OA.6 for a list of mental strategies.) By end of Grade 2, know from memory all sums of two one-digit numbers.

Use place value understanding and properties of operations to add and subtract.[4]

2.NBT.5   Fluently add and subtract within 100 using strategies based on place value, properties of operations, and/or the relationship between addition and subtraction.

---

[2] In this module, word problems focus primarily on result unknown and change unknown situations.

[3] From this point forward, fluency practice with addition and subtraction to 20 is part of the students' ongoing experience.

[4] The balance of this cluster is addressed in Modules 4 and 5.

Foundational Standards

K.OA.3   Decompose numbers less than or equal to 10 into pairs in more than one way, e.g., by using objects or drawings, and record each decomposition by a drawing or equation (e.g., 5 = 2 + 3 and 5 = 4 + 1).

K.OA.4   For any number from 1 to 9, find the number that makes 10 when added to the given number, e.g., by using objects or drawings, and record the answer with a drawing or equation.

K.NBT.1 Compose and decompose numbers from 11 to 19 into ten ones and some further ones, e.g., by using objects or drawings, and record each composition or decomposition by a drawing or equation (e.g., 18 = 10 + 8); understand that these numbers are composed of ten ones and one, two, three, four, five, six, seven, eight, or nine ones.

1.OA.6   Add and subtract within 20, demonstrating fluency for addition and subtraction within 10. Use strategies such as counting on; making ten (e.g., 8 + 6 = 8 + 2 + 4 = 10 + 4 = 14); decomposing a number leading to a ten (e.g., 13 − 4 = 13 − 3 − 1 = 10 − 1 = 9); using the relationship between addition and subtraction (e.g., knowing that 8 + 4 = 12, one knows 12 − 8 = 4); and creating equivalent but easier or known sums (e.g., adding 6 + 7 by creating the known equivalent 6 + 6 = 1 = 12 + 1 = 13).

1.NBT.4 Add within 100, including adding a two-digit number and a one-digit number, and adding a two-digit number and a multiple of 10, using concrete models or drawings and strategies based on place value, properties of operations, and/or the relationship between addition and subtraction; relate the strategy to a written method and explain the reasoning used. Understand that in adding two-digit numbers, one adds tens and tens, ones and ones; and sometimes it is necessary to compose a ten.

1.NBT.5 Given a two-digit number, mentally find 10 more or 10 less than the number, without having to count; explain the reasoning used.

1.NBT.6 Subtract multiples of 10 in the range 10–90 from multiples of 10 in the range 10–90 (positive or zero differences), using concrete models or drawings and strategies based on place value, properties of operations, and/or the relationship between addition and subtraction; relate the strategy to a written method and explain the reasoning used.

Focus Standards for Mathematical Practice

MP.1   **Make sense of problems and persevere in solving them.** Students make math drawings and use recomposing strategies to reason through the relationships in word problems. They write equations and word sentences to explain their solutions.

MP.2   **Reason abstractly and quantitatively.** Students decompose numbers and use the associative property to create equivalent but easier problems, e.g., $25 + 6 = 20 + 5 + 5 + 1$. They reason abstractly when they relate subtraction to addition and change $13 - 8 = $ ___ into an unknown addend, $8 + $ ___ $= 13$, to solve.

MP.3   **Construct viable arguments and critique the reasoning of others.** Students explain their reasoning to prove that $9 + 5 = 10 + 4$. They communicate how simpler problems embedded within more complex problems enable them to solve mentally, e.g., $8 + 3 = 11$, so $68 + 3 = 71$.

MP.7   **Look for and make use of structure.** Students use the structure of ten to add and subtract within 20, and later, within 100. E.g., $12 - 8 = 10 - 8 + 2 = 2 + 2$, and $92 + 3 = 90 + 2 + 3 = 90 + 5$.

Overview of Module Topics and Lesson Objectives

Standards	Topics and Objectives		Days
2.OA.1 **2.OA.2** K.OA.3 K.OA.4 K.NBT.1 1.OA.6	A	**Foundations for Addition and Subtraction Within 20** Lesson 1: Make number bonds of ten. Lesson 2: Make number bonds through ten with a subtraction focus and apply to one-step word problems.	2
2.OA.1 **2.OA.2**	B	**Mental Strategies for Addition and Subtraction Within 20** Lesson 3: Make a ten to add within 20. Lesson 4: Make a ten to add and subtract within 20. Lesson 5: Decompose to subtract from a ten when subtracting within 20 and apply to one-step word problems.	3
2.OA.1 **2.NBT.5** 2.OA.2 1.NBT.4 1.NBT.5 1.NBT.6	C	**Strategies for Addition and Subtraction Within 100** Lesson 6: Add and subtract within multiples of ten based on understanding place value and basic facts. Lesson 7: Add within 100 using properties of addition to make a ten. Lesson 8: Decompose to subtract from a ten when subtracting within 100 and apply to one-step word problems.	3
		End-of-Module Assessment: Topics A–C (assessment ½ day, return ½ day, remediation or further applications 1 day)	2
Total Number of Instructional Days			**10**

Terminology

Familiar Terms and Symbols

- Make ten and subtract from ten (e.g., $8 + 3 = 8 + 2 + 1$ and $15 - 7 = 10 - 7 + 5 = 3 + 5$)
- Ten plus (e.g., $10 + 3 = 13$, $30 + 5 = 35$, $70 + 8 = 78$)
- Number bond (e.g., $5 + 1 = 6$, $1 + 5 = 6$, $6 - 1 = 5$, $6 - 5 = 1$)
- Say Ten counting (e.g., 11 is "1 ten 1," 12 is "1 ten 2," twenty is "2 tens," 27 is "2 tens 7," 35 is "3 tens 5," 100 is "1 hundred," 146 is "1 hundred 4 tens 6")

Suggested Tools and Representations

- One set of ten-frame cards per student
  - One each of 1–4 and 6–9
  - Two fives
  - Ten tens
  - Blank frame
- Large set of ten-frame cards for teacher
- A bag of counters for each student (e.g., large white beans spray painted red on one side)
- Ten-strips
- Rekenrek
- Personal boards
- Hide Zero cards
- Linking cubes
- Dice

Regular	Say Ten
fifty-one	5 tens 1
sixty-seven	6 tens 7
seventy-five	7 tens 5
eighty-four	8 tens 4
ninety-five	9 tens 5

Ten-frame cards

Rekenrek

Ten-strip

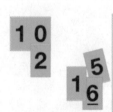

Hide Zero cards

Suggested Methods of Instructional Delivery

Directions for Administration of Sprints

Sprints are designed to develop fluency. They should be fun, adrenaline-rich activities that intentionally build energy and excitement. A fast pace is essential. During Sprint administration, teachers assume the role of athletic coaches. A rousing routine fuels students' motivation to do their personal best. Student recognition of increasing success is critical, and so every improvement is celebrated.

One Sprint has two parts with closely related problems on each. Students complete the two parts of the Sprint in quick succession with the goal of improving on the second part, even if only by one more.

With practice the following routine takes about 8 minutes.

Sprint A

Pass *Sprint A* out quickly, face down on student desks with instructions to not look at the problems until the signal is given. (Some Sprints include words. If necessary, prior to starting the Sprint quickly review the words so that reading difficulty does not slow students down.)

T: You will have 60 seconds to do as many problems as you can.

T: I do not expect you to finish all of them. Just do as many as you can, your personal best. (If some students are likely to finish before time is up, assign a number to *count by* on the back.)

T: Take your mark! Get set! THINK! (When you say THINK, students turn their papers over and work furiously to finish as many problems as they can in 60 seconds. Time precisely.)

After 60 seconds:

T: Stop! Circle the last problem you did. I will read just the answers. If you got it right, call out "Yes!" and give a fist pump. If you made a mistake, circle it. Ready?

T: (Energetically, rapid-fire call the first answer.)

S: Yes!

T: (Energetically, rapid-fire call the second answer.)

S: Yes!

Repeat to the end of *Sprint A*, or until no one has any more correct. If need be, read the *count by* answers in the same way you read Sprint answers. Each number *counted by* on the back is considered a correct answer.

T: Fantastic! Now write the number you got correct at the top of your page. This is your personal goal for Sprint B.

T: How many of you got 1 right? (All hands should go up.)

T: Keep your hand up until I say the number that is 1 more than the number you got right. So, if you got 14 correct, when I say 15 your hand goes down. Ready?

T: (Quickly.) How many got 2 correct? 3? 4? 5? (Continue until all hands are down.)

Optional routine, depending on whether or not your class needs more practice with *Sprint A*:

T: I'll give you one minute to do more problems on this half of the Sprint. If you finish, stand behind your chair. (As students work you might have the person who scored highest on *Sprint A* pass out *Sprint B*.)

T: Stop! I will read just the answers. If you got it right, call out "Yes!" and give a fist pump. If you made a mistake, circle it. Ready? (Read the answers to the first half again as students stand.)

Movement

To keep the energy and fun going, always do a stretch or a movement game in between Sprint A and B. For example, the class might do jumping jacks while skip counting by 5 for about 1 minute. Feeling invigorated, students take their seats for *Sprint B,* ready to make every effort to complete more problems this time.

Sprint B

Pass *Sprint B* out quickly, face down on student desks with instructions to not look at the problems until the signal is given. (Repeat the procedure for *Sprint A* up through the show of hands for how many right.)

T: Stand up if you got more correct on the second Sprint than on the first.

S: (Students stand.)

T: Keep standing until I say the number that tells how many more you got right on Sprint B. So if you got 3 more right on Sprint B than you did on Sprint A, when I say 3 you sit down. Ready? (Call out numbers starting with 1. Students sit as the number by which they improved is called. Celebrate the students who improved most with a cheer.)

T: Well done! Now take a moment to go back and correct your mistakes. Think about what patterns you noticed in today's Sprint.

T: How did the patterns help you get better at solving the problems?

T: Rally Robin your thinking with your partner for 1 minute. Go!

Rally Robin is a style of sharing in which partners trade information back and forth, one statement at a time per person, for about 1 minute. This is an especially valuable part of the routine for students who benefit from their friends' support to identify patterns and try new strategies.

Students may take Sprints home.

Personal Boards

Materials Needed for Personal Boards

1 High Quality Clear Sheet Protector
1 piece of stiff red tag board 11" x 8 ¼"
1 piece of stiff white tag board 11" x 8 ¼"
1 3"x 3" piece of dark synthetic cloth for an eraser
1 Low Odor Blue Dry Erase Marker: Fine Point

Directions for Creating Personal Boards

Cut your white and red tag to specifications. Slide into the sheet protector. Store your eraser on the red side. Store markers in a separate container to avoid stretching the sheet protector.

Frequently Asked Questions About Personal Boards

Why is one side red and one white?

> The white side of the board is the "paper." Students generally write on it and if working individually then turn the board over to signal to the teacher they have completed their work. The teacher then says, "Show me your boards," when most of the class is ready.

What are some of the benefits of a personal board?

- The teacher can respond quickly to a hole in student understandings and skills. "Let's do some of these on our personal boards until we have more mastery."

- Student can erase quickly so that they do not have to suffer the evidence of their mistake.

- They are motivating. Students love both the drill and thrill capability and the chance to do story problems with an engaging medium.

- Checking work gives the teacher instant feedback about student understanding.

What is the benefit of this personal board over a commercially purchased dry erase board?

- It is much less expensive.

- Templates such as place value charts, number bond mats, hundreds boards, and number lines can be stored between the two pieces of tag for easy access and reuse.

- Worksheets, story problems, and other problem sets can be done without marking the paper so that students can work on the problems independently at another time.

- Strips with story problems, number lines, and arrays can be inserted and still have a full piece of paper to write on.

- The red versus white side distinction clarifies your expectations. When working collaboratively, there is no need to use the red. When working independently, the students know how to keep their work private.

- The sheet protector can be removed so that student work can be projected on an overhead.

Scaffolds[5]

The scaffolds integrated into *A Story of Units* give alternatives for how students access information as well as express and demonstrate their learning. Strategically placed margin notes are provided within each lesson elaborating on the use of specific scaffolds at applicable times. They address many needs presented by English language learners, students with disabilities, students performing above grade level, and students performing below grade level. Many of the suggestions are organized by Universal Design for Learning (UDL) principles and are applicable to more than one population. To read more about the approach to differentiated instruction in *A Story of Units,* please refer to "How to Implement *A Story of Units.*"

Assessment Summary

Type	Administered	Format	Standards Addressed
End-of-Module Assessment Task	After Topic C	Constructed response with rubric	2.OA.1 2.OA.2 2.NBT.5

---

[5] Students with disabilities may require Braille, large print, audio, or special digital files. Please visit the website, www.p12.nysed.gov/specialed/aim, for specific information on how to obtain student materials that satisfy the National Instructional Materials Accessibility Standard (NIMAS) format.

GRADE 2 • MODULE 1

Topic A

Foundations for Addition and Subtraction Within 20

2.OA.1, **2.OA.2**, K.OA.3, K.OA.4, K.NBT.1, 1.OA.6

Focus Standards:	2.OA.1	Use addition and subtraction within 100 to solve one- and two-step word problems involving situations of adding to, taking from, putting together, taking apart, and comparing, with unknowns in all positions, e.g., by using drawings and equations with a symbol for the unknown number to represent the problem.
	2.OA.2	Fluently add and subtract within 20 using mental strategies. By end of Grade 2, know from memory all sums of two one-digit numbers.
Instructional Days:	2	
Coherence -Links from:	G1–M2	Introduction to Place Value Through Addition and Subtraction Within 20
-Links to:	G2–M4	Addition and Subtraction Within 200 with Word Problems to 100
	G3–M2	Place Value and Problem Solving with Units of Measure

In this first module of Grade 2, students make significant progress towards fluency with sums and differences within 20 (**2.OA.2**). Fluency, coupled with a fundamental grasp of place value, rests on three essential skills: 1) knowing number bonds of ten, 2) adding ten and some ones, and 3) the number bonds (pairs) of numbers through ten. Topic A energetically revisits this familiar ground from kindergarten (**K.OA.3**) and Grade 1 (**1.OA.6**) at a new pace; we move quickly from concrete to pictorial to abstract. All the material included herein can be included in daily fluency work, and should be if students lack fluency with mental strategies.

In Lesson 1, students use ten-frames to model number bonds of ten as they generate addition and subtraction number sentences and solve for the missing part by bonding, counting on, or subtracting. Students record and share number bonds of 10 to regain their Grade 1 fluency and understanding. Lesson 2 continues with students revisiting number pairs through 10 and each pair's related facts. Again, students work with ten-frame cards to create number bonds and to determine a corresponding subtraction number sentence. As students play a part–whole game, they practice finding the missing part and decomposing a given quantity in a variety of ways.

The application problems in these earlier lessons follow the concept development to provide students with the opportunity to discover the connection between the one-step story problems **(2.OA.1)** and the models (i.e., ten-frames, number bonds) and to articulate their observations with classmates.

A Teaching Sequence Towards Mastery of Foundations for Addition and Subtraction Within 20

Objective 1: Make number bonds of ten.
(Lesson 1)

Objective 2: Make number bonds through ten with a subtraction focus and apply to one-step word problems.
(Lesson 2)

Lesson 1

Objective: Make number bonds of ten.

Suggested Lesson Structure

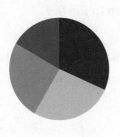

■ Fluency Practice	(19 minutes)
■ Concept Development	(16 minutes)
■ Application Problems	(15 minutes)
■ Student Debrief	(10 minutes)
Total Time	**(60 minutes)**

Fluency Practice (19 minutes)

- Happy Counting 1–10 **2.NBT.2**   (2 minutes)
- Break 10 in 2 Parts **2.OA.2**   (5 minutes)
- Add Tens and Some Ones **2.OA.2**   (12 minutes)

Happy Counting 1–10 (2 minutes)

Note: On the first day, counting up and down to 10 simply alerts students to the fun and challenge of changing direction and establishing a protocol that will quickly advance to larger numbers as the module unfolds.

Make your hand motions emphatic so the students' counting is sharp and crisp. Once students get the hang of it, make the counting more challenging by skip-counting or starting at higher numbers. Also, it's *Happy Counting*, not *Happy Mouth*, so resist the urge to mouth the answers. Students need to do the work, so they have to watch your fingers!

- T: We're going to play a game called Happy Counting!
- T: Watch my hand to know whether to count up or down. A closed hand means stop. (Show signals as you explain.)
- T: Let's count by ones, starting at zero. Ready? (Teacher rhythmically points up until a change is desired. Show a closed hand then point down. Continue, mixing it up.)
- S: 0, 1, 2, 3, (stop), 2, 1, 0, (stop), 1, 2, 3, 4, 5, (stop), 4, 3, 2, 1, 0, (stop), 1, 2, 3, 4, 5, 6, 7, (stop), 6, 5, 4, (stop), 5, 6, 7, 8, 9, 10, (stop), 9, 8, 7, 6.
- T: Excellent! Try it for 30 seconds with your partner. Partner A, you are the teacher today.

COMMON CORE™

Lesson 1:   Make number bonds of ten.
Date: 6/25/13

1.A.3

Break 10 in 2 Parts (5 minutes)

Materials: (S) One stick of ten linking cubes with a color change after the fifth cube

Note: There is almost no foundational skill more important than fluency with the bonds of numbers within 10. By starting at the concrete level, students quickly re-engage with their hopefully hard-wired knowledge of their bonds of 10. The color change also orients them to the five.

  T: Now let's play Break 10 in 2 Parts
  T: Show me your 10 stick. (Students show.) Hide it behind your back.
  T: I will say the size of one part. Break that part off in one piece. Then without peeking, see if you know how many are in the other part.
  T: Ready?
  S: Yes!
  T: Break off 2. No peeking. At the signal, tell how many are in the other part. (Give signal.)
  S: 8!
  T: Show your parts and see if you are correct.
  S: It's 8!
  T: What parts are you holding?
  S: 2 and 8.
  T: What's the whole?
  S: 10.

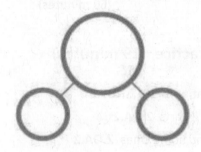

Continue with the following possible sequences: 3 and 7, 1 and 9, 4 and 6, 5 and 5. Show the bond (as pictured to the right) and continue with the remaining bonds at an ever-quickening pace.

  T: Turn and talk to your partner about how this game is the same or different than one you played in first grade.
  T: How did knowing that help you play today?
  T: Tell your partner which pattern or strategy helped you to find the missing part when you couldn't peek at how many were left.

Sprint: Add Tens and Some Ones (12 minutes)

Materials: (S) Add Tens and Some Ones Sprint

Note: This particular choice brings automaticity back with the Ten Plus sums, foundational for the *make a ten* strategy and expanded form.

NOTES ON MULTIPLE MEANS OF ACTION AND EXPRESSION:

For sprints, a fast pace is essential and builds energy and excitement. To support students who don't excel under pressure, you may give them the chance to practice the sprint at home the night before it is administered.

To maintain a high level of energy and enthusiasm, always do a stretch or a movement game in between Sprint A and Sprint B. For example, do jumping jacks while skip-counting by fives.

Lesson 1:   Make number bonds of ten.
Date: 6/25/13

1.A.4

Directions for Administration of Sprints

One sprint has two parts with closely related problems on each. The problems on each part move from simple to complex, creating a challenge for every learner. Before the lesson, cut the sprint sheet in half to create Sprint A and Sprint B. Students complete the two parts of the sprint in quick succession with the goal of improving on the second part, even if only by one more. With practice the following routine takes about 8 minutes.

Sprint A

(Put Sprint A face down on desks with instructions to not look at problems until the signal is given.)

- T: You will have 60 seconds to do as many problems as you can.
- T: I do not expect you to finish all of them. Just do as many as you can, your personal best.
- T: Take your mark! Get set! THINK! (When you say THINK, students turn papers over and work furiously to finish as many problems as they can in 60 seconds. Time precisely.)

(After 60 seconds:)

- T: Stop! Circle the last problem you did. I will read just the answers. If you got it right, call out "Yes!" and give a fist pump. If you made a mistake, circle it. Ready?

(Repeat to the end of Sprint A or until no one has any more correct.)

- T: Now write your correct number at the top of the page. This is your personal goal for Sprint B.
- T: How many of you got 1 right? (All hands should go up.)
- T: Keep your hand up until I say a number that is 1 more than the number you got right. So, if you got 14 right, when I say 15 your hand goes down. Ready?
- T: (Quickly.) How many got 2 right? And 3, 4, 5, etc. (Continue until all hands are down.)

(Optional routine, depending on whether or not the class needs more practice with Sprint A.)

- T: Take one minute to do more problems on this half of the sprint.

(As students work, you might have the person who scored highest on Sprint A pass out Sprint B.)

- T: Stop! I will read just answers. If you got it right, call out "Yes!" and give a fist pump. If you made a mistake, circle it. Ready? (Read the answers to the first half again.)

Note: To keep the energy and fun going, do a stretch or a movement game in between sprints.

Sprint B

(Put Sprint B face down on desks with instructions to not look at the problems until the signal is given. Repeat the procedure for Sprint A up through the show of hands for how many right.)

- T: Stand up if you got more correct on the second sprint than on the first.
- S: (Students stand.)
- T: Keep standing until I say the number that tells how many more you got right on Sprint B. If you got 3 more right on Sprint B than on Sprint A, when I say 3 you sit down. Ready?

(Call out numbers starting with 1. Students sit as the number by which they improved is called.)

An alternate method is to choose three students to tell how many they got correct on Sprint A and Sprint B.

| Lesson 1: | Make number bonds of ten. |
| Date: | 6/25/13 |

1.A.5

For each set of scores, on your signal, the class chorally says the difference. This provides frequent practice with counting on and other mental strategies, and it reinforces the relationship between addition and subtraction.

T: Miguel, how many did you get correct on Sprint A and Sprint B?

S: On Sprint A, I got 12, and on Sprint B I got 17.

T: How many more did Miguel do on Sprint B than on Sprint A? (Pause.)

S: (Students respond chorally.) 5!

Students may take sprints home.

Concept Development (16 minutes)

Materials: (T) Large set of ten-frame cards in the following suggested order: 5, 9, 1, 8, 2, 7, 3, 6, 4, 5, 10
(S) Personal white boards, deck of eleven ten-frame cards that show the numbers 1–10, with an extra card that shows 5 (see image below)

Note: This activity provides visual support as it invites students to remember the number bonds of 10.

T: Place your ten-frame cards in order from largest to smallest.

T: Move your ten-frames that have 5 or fewer dots to make ten (see model).

S: (Students move cards, placing the 1 on the 9, etc.)

T: Now go through your bonds of 10 out loud: (10 and 0, 9 and 1, 8 and 2, 7 and 3, etc.)

T: Close your eyes and see if you can remember them without looking.

T: Open your eyes and do it again. Who got better at their number bonds of 10?

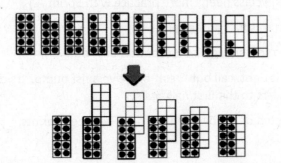

Note: This next activity requires students to visualize (for those who still need support) or recall from memory (for those who achieved mastery of partners to 10) the missing addend. It also refreshes their subitizing skills, as students only have a few seconds to recognize the set of 5 and the set of 2 on the image below as 7, in order to complete the number sentence.

T: Here is a ten-frame card. Tell me the addition sentence to make ten. Wait for the signal. (Flash a ten-frame dot card for about two seconds.)

S: 7 + 3 = 10, 5 + 5 = 10, 9 + 1 = 10, 8 + 2 = 10, etc.

T: This time, tell me the subtraction sentence to get to the number of dots shown.

| Lesson 1: | Make number bonds of ten. |
| Date: | 6/25/13 |

1.A.6

Wait for the signal. (Flash a ten-frame dot card for about two seconds.)

S: 10 − 7 = 3, 10 − 5 = 5, 10 − 9 = 1, 10 − 1 = 9, etc.

T: Partner A: Turn over your ten-frame cards to hide the dots.
  1. Show the top card for two seconds.
  2. Wait for your partner to tell you the addition sentence and subtraction sentence.
  3. Flash the next card.
  4. Keep going until the buzzer sounds after one minute.

T: (Set the timer for one minute.) Partner B, do the same.

T: Let's try the class set again. (Repeat the class set. Give verbal praise specific to observed improvement, "Students, you really improved at making 10 from 2, 3, and 4, which have always been a greater challenge.")

T: Partners, talk about how 6 + 4 helps you solve 10 − 6.

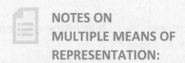

NOTES ON MULTIPLE MEANS OF REPRESENTATION:

Post the first few problems of each set on the board, so students can identify the pattern. Underline, highlight, or use a different color for the digits in the ones place to draw attention to making a ten.

Call out one number for students to show with their fingers. They show the missing part and say the number sentence.

T: Four.

S: (Students show 4 fingers. Then they show 6.) 4 + 6 = 10.

T: (Continue quickly through the remaining partners to 10.)

For three minutes, students write number bonds of 10 on personal boards or blank paper without pictures or manipulatives. If they get stuck, invite them to visualize ten-frame cards rather than use them. Close by having partners share their work and look for commonalities. (Template included.)

Once having generated the pairs independently in writing, briefly continue forward into teen numbers with addition, numbers to 40, and numbers to 100 as students are able. This adds excitement as students see their sums applying to bigger numbers. Keep a lively pace.

MP.2

T: 5 + 5 is?

S: 10.

T: 15 + 5 is?

S: 20!

T: 25 + 5 is?

T: 30!

T: 65 + 5 is?

S: 70.

Repeat the process as time allows, possibly using the following sequence: 7 + 3, 17 + 3, 27 + 3, 57 + 3; 8 + 2, 28 + 2, and 48 + 2.

| Lesson 1: | Make number bonds of ten. |
| Date: | 6/25/13 |

1.A.7

Application Problems (15 minutes)

Problem 1

Mrs. Potter paints her fingernails one at a time from left to right. If she paints 1 fingernail, how many fingernails will she have unpainted? How many other combinations of painted and unpainted nails can she have?

		1 and 9	4 + 6
		2 and 8	5 + 5
		3 and 7	6 + 4
			7 + 3
They are partners			8 + 2
to 10!			9 + 1

Problem 2

The cashier puts exactly 10 bills inside each envelope. How many more bills does he need to put in each of the following envelopes?

   a.   An envelope with 9 bills. (1)

   b.   An envelope with 5 bills. (5)

   c.   An envelope with 1 bill. (9)

   d.   Find other numbers of bills that might be in an envelope and tell how many more bills the cashier needs to put to make 10 bills.

A different cashier puts exactly 30 bills in each envelope. How many more bills does he need to put in each of the following envelopes?

   a.   An envelope with 28 bills. (2)

   b.   An envelope with 22 bills. (8)

   c.   An envelope with 24 bills. (6)

Note: Choose one or both problems based on the needs of your students and the time constraint of 15 minutes. These problems are designed to elicit connections between the fingernails, envelopes, and ten-frames, which can be explored during the Debrief. 15 minutes have been allotted in order for you to review the Read, Draw, Write (RDW) Process for problem-solving.

Directions on the RDW Process: Read the problem, draw and label, write a number sentence, and write a word sentence. The more students participate in reasoning through problems with a systematic approach, the more they internalize those behaviors and thought processes.

(Excerpted from "How to Implement A Story of Units.")

Problem Set

Students should do their personal best to complete the Problem Set within the allotted 10 minutes. Some problems do not specify a method for solving. This is an intentional reduction of scaffolding that invokes MP.5, Use Appropriate Tools Strategically. Students should solve these problems using the RDW approach used for Application Problems.

For some classes, it may be appropriate to modify the assignment by specifying which problems students should work on first. With this option, let the careful sequencing of the problem set guide your selections so that problems continue to scaffold. Balance word problems with other problem types to ensure a range of practice. Assign incomplete problems for homework or at another time during the day.

Student Debrief (10 minutes)

Lesson Objective: Make number bonds of ten.

The Student Debrief is intended to invite reflection and active processing of the total lesson experience.

Invite students to review their solutions for the Problem Set. They should check work by comparing answers with a partner before going over answers as a class. Look for misconceptions or misunderstandings that can be addressed in the Debrief. Guide students in a conversation to debrief the Problem Set and process the lesson. You may choose to use any combination of the questions below to lead the discussion.

- Compare the envelope problem to the fingernail problem. What is different about the problems? What is the same about them?

- (Hold up a ten-frame card). Why do you think I chose to use the ten-frame cards today?

- (Hold up the ten-stick of linking cubes with the color change after the fifth cube.) How does the color change at the five help us with learning our bonds of ten?

- Instead of a color change, how does the ten-frame show the five?

- How did the first envelope problem help you solve the second one? How does 6 + 4 help you to solve 26 + 4?

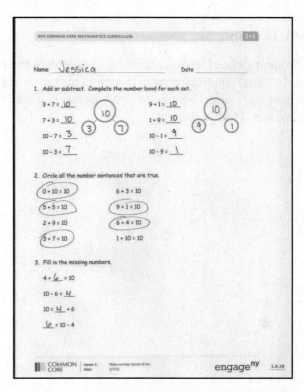

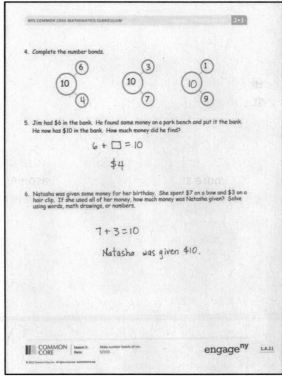

COMMON CORE

Lesson 1:   Make number bonds of ten.
Date: 6/25/13

1.A.9

© 2013 Common Core, Inc. All rights reserved. **commoncore.org**

Exit Ticket (3 minutes)

After the Student Debrief, instruct students to complete the Exit Ticket. A review of their work will help you assess the students' understanding of the concepts that were presented in the lesson today and plan more effectively for future lessons. You may read the questions aloud to the students.

Do as many as you can in 60 seconds.

#		#	
1	10 + 1 =	16	10 and 1 make ____
2	10 + 2 =	17	2 more than 10 is ____
3	10 + 4 =	18	10 and 0 make ____
4	10 + 3 =	19	10 and 3 make ____
5	10 + 5 =	20	10 and 6 make ____
6	10 + 6 =	21	1 more than 10 is ____
7	10 + 0 =	22	10 and 4 make ____
8	10 + 7 =	23	10 and 5 make ____
9	10 + 9 =	24	10 and 9 make ____
10	10 + 10 =	25	10 and 6 make ____
11	10 + 1 =	26	6 more than 10 is ____
12	10 + 3 =	27	10 and 10 make ____
13	10 + 4 =	28	3 more than 10 is ____
14	10 + 2 =	29	10 and 2 make ____
15	10 + 3 =	30	2 more than 10 is ____

Do you know your 10 pluses?

Do as many as you can in 60 seconds.

#		#	
1	10 + 3 =	16	10 and 3 make ____
2	10 + 4 =	17	4 more than 10 is ____
3	10 + 1 =	18	10 and 4 make ____
4	10 + 2 =	19	10 and 2 make ____
5	10 + 3 =	20	10 and 1 make ____
6	10 + 4 =	21	3 more than 10 is ____
7	10 + 1 =	22	10 and 4 make ____
8	10 + 2 =	23	10 and 2 make ____
9	10 + 3 =	24	10 and 8 make ____
10	10 + 4 =	25	7 more than 10 is ____
11	10 + 1 =	26	10 and 9 make ____
12	10 + 2 =	27	10 and 0 make ____
13	10 + 3 =	28	3 more than 10 is ____
14	10 + 1 =	29	10 and 2 make ____
15	10 + 2 =	30	5 more than 10 is ____

Robin Ramos 2005

Name _____   Date _____

1. Add or subtract. Complete the number bond for each set.

3 + 7 = ____   9 + 1 = ____

7 + 3 = ____   1 + 9 = ____

10 – 7 = ____   10 – 1 = ____

10 – 3 = ____   10 – 9 = ____

2. Circle all the number sentences that are true.

0 + 10 = 10   6 + 3 = 10

5 + 5 = 10   9 + 1 = 10

2 + 9 = 10   6 + 4 = 10

3 + 7 = 10   1 + 10 = 10

3. Fill in the missing numbers.

4 + ____ = 10

10 – 6 = ____

10 = ____ + 6

____ = 10 – 4

COMMON CORE™   Lesson 1:   Make number bonds of ten.
                 Date: 6/25/13

1.A.12

4. Complete the number bonds.

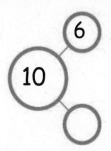   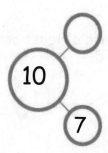   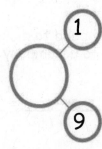

5. Jim had $6 in the bank. He found some money on a park bench and put it the bank. He now has $10 in the bank. How much money did he find?

6. Natasha was given some money for her birthday. She spent $7 on a bow and $3 on a hair clip. If she used all of her money, how much money was Natasha given? Solve using words, math drawings, or numbers.

Name _____   Date _____

Complete each number bond to make 10. Write at least one addition and one subtraction sentence to accompany each bond.

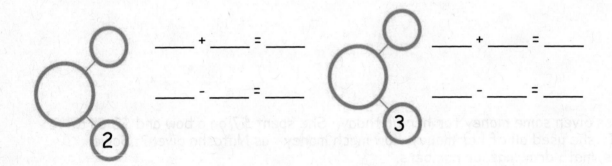

____ + ____ = ____

____ - ____ = ____

____ + ____ = ____

____ - ____ = ____

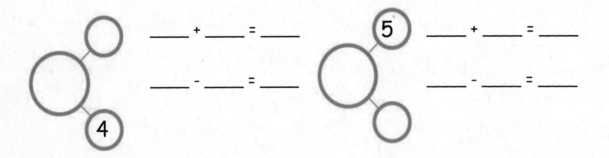

____ + ____ = ____

____ - ____ = ____

____ + ____ = ____

____ - ____ = ____

____ + ____ = ____

____ - ____ = ____

____ + ____ = ____

____ - ____ = ____

COMMON CORE™ | Lesson 1: Make number bonds of ten.
Date: 6/25/13

1.A.14

Name _____   Date _____

1. Circle all number sentences that are true.

     6 + 4 = 10   5 + 5 = 1 + 9

     10 = 3 + 7   2 + 8 = 7 + 3

     10 - 7 = 4   8 - 2 = 10

2. Add or Subtract.

     10 - 7= _____

     8 + 2 = _____

     10 - 5 = _____

     3 + 7 = _____

     10 - 0= _____

3. Solve the problems.

     1 + 9 =   59 + 1 =

     15 + 5 =   65 + 5 =

     28 + 2 =   72 + 8 =

     33 + 7 =   87 + 3 =

     46 + 4 =   94 + 6 =

4. Complete the number bonds.

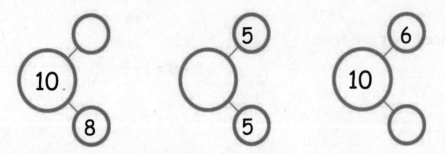

5. Your little brother has $4 and wants to spend the money on an action figure that costs $10. How much money does he still need to buy the action figure?

6. Daniel found $14. His father gave him some more. Then he had $20. How much money was he given? Write a number sentence to show your thinking.

7. Amy read 24 books. Peter read 30 books. Amy wants to read as many books as Peter. Amy thinks she needs to read 7 more books to reach her goal. Is she right? Explain using words, math drawings, or numbers.

Name _____   Date _____

Draw all the number bonds of 10. The first one is done for you.

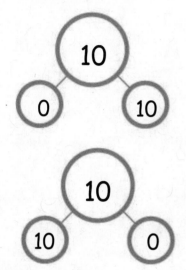

Lesson 2

Objective: Make number bonds through ten with a subtraction focus and apply to one-step word problems.

Suggested Lesson Structure

■ Fluency Practice	(15 minutes)
■ Concept Development	(20 minutes)
■ Application Problems	(15 minutes)
■ Student Debrief	(10 minutes)
Total Time	**(60 minutes)**

Fluency Practice (15 minutes)

- Happy Counting 9–25 **2.NBT.2**   (2 minutes)
- Say Ten Counting from 5 to 25 **2.NBT.1**   (6 minutes)
- Ten Plus Number Sentences **2.OA.2**   (3 minutes)
- Make Ten by Identifying the Missing Part **2.OA.2**   (4 minutes)

Happy Counting 9–25 (2 minutes)

Note: Students practice fluently crossing the ten on day 2, meaning they work up and down especially focusing on 8, 9, 10, 11, 12, 11, 10, 9, 8 and 18, 19, 20, 21, 22, 21, 20, 19, 18.

     T: We're going to play a game called Happy Counting!

     T: Watch my hand to know whether to count up or down. A closed hand means stop. (Show signals as you explain.)

     T: Let's count by ones, starting at zero. Ready? (Rhythmically point up until a change is desired. Show a closed hand then point down. Continue, mixing it up.)

     S: 9, 10, 11, 12, 13, 14 (stop) 13, 12, 11 (stop) 12, 13, 14, 15, 16, 17, 18 (stop) 17, 16, 15, 14 (stop) 15, 16, 17, 18, 19, 20 (stop) 19, 18, 17 (stop) 18, 19, 20, 21, 22, 23 (stop) 22, 21, 20, 19 (stop) 20, 21, 22, 23, 24, 25.

     T: Excellent! Try it for 30 seconds with your partner. Partner B, you are the teacher today.

Say Ten Counting from 5 to 25 (6 minutes)

Note: Research substantiates that unit form counting, or counting the Say Ten way, supports number sense in that the naming of the numbers reveals the base ten to students. Students have been counting this way since kindergarten.

Lesson 2:	Make number bonds through ten with a subtraction focus and apply to one-step word problems.
Date:	6/25/13

Hide Zero cards and the Rekenrek (both pictured below) beautifully parallel Say Ten counting.

- T: The Say Ten way to say 11 is 1 ten 1. (Pull the cards apart to show the 10 and the 1.) In Say Ten counting, we first state the number of tens and then state the number of ones.
- T: (Show 12 with place value cards.) 2 more than 10, not in Say Ten way?
- S: 12
- T: (Pull cards apart.) The Say Ten way is to say 12?
- S: 1 ten 2
- T: (Show 13.) What is the Say Ten way for 13?
- S: 1 ten 3
- T: (Pull cards apart.) Yes!
- T: Let's count the Say Ten way, starting from 5 on the Rekenrek. As I move the beads, count aloud.

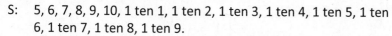

Beads on the Rekenrek start out pushed to the right. To show 5, a row of 5 are pulled to the left. To show 1 ten 1, a row of ten and a second row of one are pulled to the left, etc.

- S: 5, 6, 7, 8, 9, 10, 1 ten 1, 1 ten 2, 1 ten 3, 1 ten 4, 1 ten 5, 1 ten 6, 1 ten 7, 1 ten 8, 1 ten 9.
- T: 2 tens (show two rows of ten beads pulled to the left), and the pattern begins again.
- S: 2 tens 1, 2 tens 2, 2 tens 3, 2 tens 4, 2 tens 5.
- T: Partner B, tell your partner what patterns you noticed as you counted numbers 11–19.
- T: Talk with your partner about how Say Ten counting numbers 11–19 relates to counting numbers 20–29.

Ten Plus Number Sentences (3 minutes)

Materials: (T) Ten-frame cards, Hide Zero cards

Note: Students should be able to claim proficiency with their *ten plus* facts. "My ten-plus facts are easy! I just know them. 10 + 9 is 19. See I didn't have to count." Clearly this then extends into knowing 20 + 9 and later understanding expanded form without difficulty.

- T: I will flash two ten-frame cards, ten and another card. Wait for the signal. Then tell me the addition sentence that combines the numbers. Let's say numbers the regular way.
- T: (Flash 10 and 5.)
- S: 10 + 5 = 15.

Continue with the following possible sequence: 10 and 9, 10 and 1, 10 and 3.

- T: Let's use Hide Zero cards for larger numbers. (Flash 30 and 5.)

Continue with the following possible sequence: 30 and 8, 70 and 8, 70 and 7

| Lesson 2: | Make number bonds through ten with a subtraction focus and apply to one-step word problems. |
| Date: | 6/25/13 |

1.A.19

T: Talk to your partner about 10 + 8 = 18, 30 + 8 = 38 and 70 + 8 = 78. (Write these facts on the board.) What is the same about these facts? What is different?

T: Partner A, explain how one problem helps you solve the other.

T: Partner B, explain how Say Ten counting is like *ten plus* number sentences.

Make Ten by Identifying the Missing Part (4 minutes)

Materials: (S) Personal white boards

Note: Students need this skill as they add 8 and 6 using the ten and subsequently add 18 and 6 or 80 and 60.

T: If I say 9, you say 1 because 9 needs 1 to be 10.

T: Wait for the signal, 5.

S: 5.

Continue with the following possible sequence: 8, 2, 9, 1.

T: This time I'll say a number and you write the addition sentence to make ten on your personal white board.

T: 0. Get ready. Show me your board.

S: 0 + 10 = 10.

T: 10. Get ready. Show me your board.

S: 10 + 0 = 10.

Continue with the following possible sequence: 3, 7, 6, 4.

T: Turn and explain to your partner what pattern you noticed that helped you solve the problems.

S: First you said 0 and the answer was 0 + 10 = 10; next you said 10 and the answer was 10 + 0 = 10. The numbers switched places!

Concept Development (20 minutes)

Materials: (T) Set of ten-frame cards (S) Per pair of students: set of ten-frame cards, ten two-sided counters, a blank ten-frame, a die, a hiding paper, personal white boards

Note: This lesson builds on the previous lesson as students reestablish their Grade 1 mastery of sums and differences to 10. The focus is on subtraction facts since, in general, students are proficient in addition but often mistakenly write 2 − 7 = 5, for example, rather than 7 − 2 = 5.

T: Look at the card I'm holding up. (Hold up a ten-frame with 6 dots.)

T: How many dots do you see?

S: 6.

T: In your mind, subtract 1. At the signal tell me the subtraction sentence. Wait for my signal.

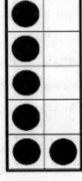

COMMON CORE™   Lesson 2:   Make number bonds through ten with a subtraction focus and apply   1.A.20
                    to one-step word problems.
          Date: 6/25/13

© 2013 Common Core, Inc. All rights reserved. commoncore.org

S: 6 − 1 = 5.

T: Good. Let's keep going. As you look at the 6 card, subtract the number I tell you. Wait for the signal. 5. (Signal.)

S: 6 − 5 = 1.

T: Nice work! (Keep going, subtracting 2, 4, 3, and 0 before advancing to the 7 card with a similar sequence.)

T: (Hold up a ten-frame with 7 dots.) Now how many dots do you see?

S: 7.

T: (Continue through the bonds of 7.)

T: Now, you practice in pairs using the 8 and 9 cards to quiz each other. Partner A, you start with the 8 card. When I say to switch, Partner B will start quizzing partner A with the 9 card.

T: (Pass out materials for the following activity: ten two-sided counters, a blank ten-frame, a die, a blank piece of paper to hide the counters.)

T: I will tell you the whole amount. Partner B shows the whole using counters on the ten-frame.

T: If I say that the whole is 7, Partner B shows one color of 7 counters on the ten-frame.

T: Now Partner A, roll the die to determine the part to change color. What part did you roll?

S: 4.

T: Hiding all the counters from Partner A, Partner B flips 4 counters to the other color.

T: Partner A, say the subtraction sentence to find the part that didn't change color.

S: 7 − 4 = 3. The part that didn't change color is 3!

T: Partner B, show the counters to prove whether Partner A is correct or incorrect.

T: Continue playing for 30 seconds. I will then say switch. Exchange materials. As I watch and listen to you work and improve, I will pass you on to the next larger number when you are ready. (Move students on to wholes of 8, 9, 10 and beyond.)

Note: Conduct a short debriefing to give students time to reflect and share insights.

T: There are some problems that you may do more slowly than others. Which ones slow you down?

S: Subtracting 6 from 9 is hard for me.

T: Who can share a way they subtract 6 from 9 with the class?

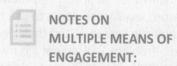

NOTES ON MULTIPLE MEANS OF ENGAGEMENT:

Choose one or both application problems based on the needs of your students and the time constraint of 15 minutes.

Take care that the connection between the concept development and the application problems is not made too explicit; the goal is for students to discover these connections: "Oh! This is just *ten plus* number sentences!" "I can use what I practiced in *make 10* to do the apples problem!" Ask questions to probe what students mean and encourage them to articulate their observations, especially during the Debrief when you want the lesson's objective to become eminently clear to the students.

Lesson 2:   Make number bonds through ten with a subtraction focus and apply to one-step word problems.

Date: 6/25/13

1.A.21

S: My fives are easy for me. 9 – 5 is 4 so 9 – 6 is one less, 3. → I think, 6 plus what is 9? I know that is
      3. → I know my tens. 10 – 6 is 4 so 9 – 6 is one less. → I know my number pairs. 6 and 3 is 9 so 9 –
      6 is 3.

T: Partner B, turn and talk to your partner about one strategy you just heard and understood that is
      different from the one you used. (Pause.) Partner A, take a turn.

Application Problems (15 minutes)

Problem 1

There are both red and green apples in a bag. (Select a total number of apples as appropriate for your
students. Be sure your students are proficient with 7, 8, and 9 before choosing a larger number.) How many
red and how many green apples might there be in the bag?

Problem 2

Sherry already has 10 stickers. Now her goal is to collect 20 in
all. She got 4 more on Monday and 4 again on Tuesday.

- How many does she have in all?
- How many more does she need to make her goal?
- How many does she need if her goal is to collect 30
  stickers?

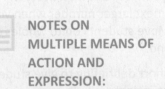

Note: Problem 1 relates to the fingernail problem from the
previous day's lesson. Instruct students to use the RDW
procedure (introduced in Lesson 1) and their personal white
boards to complete Problem 1. Problem 2 is more
challenging, and the goal is for students to do their best within the allotted time (time-frame), not to
complete all tasks (task-frame). The two problems create a differentiation opportunity. Those students who
grasp the concept can move on, while those who need more practice can work on Problem 1.

Guide students through the problem by rereading it and then
drawing and labeling each piece of information as it is given.
(Be sure students write the equation and the statement of the
answer for each part as it is solved on their personal white
boards.) This systematic approach will support students as they
work independently on the Problem Set and at home.

T: Let's read Problem 2 together through Part (a).
S: (Students read chorally.)
T: Tell your partner what you see when you hear the
      story.
S: (Students share with partners.)
T: What can you draw to show Part (a)?

**NOTES ON
MULTIPLE MEANS OF
ACTION AND
EXPRESSION:**

As you circulate during this Application
lesson segment, identify a student who
uses an efficient representation or
strategy. Ask the student to share her
work with the class during the Student
Debrief. Select work that advances
efficient ways of counting and grouping
rather than work that shows scattered
representations.

Lesson 2:   Make number bonds through ten with a subtraction focus and apply
             to one-step word problems.
Date: 6/25/13

1.A.22

S: A page with 10 stickers, and then another page that's getting fuller because she got stickers on Monday and stickers on Tuesday. → 10 stickers and 8 more.

T: I'll give you two minutes to make your drawing of the story.

T: Explain to your partner what your drawing shows.

T: (Wait until a brief exchange is complete.) How many stickers does Sherry have now?

S: 18.

T: 18 what? It's important to always state the unit.

S: 18 stickers.

T: Turn and tell your partner what number sentence you can write to show your drawing.

At this point continue through the process of having the students write the equation and the statement of the answer.

Problem Set (10 minutes)

Students should do their personal best to complete the Problem Set within the allotted 10 minutes. For some classes, it may be appropriate to modify the assignment by specifying which problems they work on first. Some problems do not specify a method for solving. Students solve these problems using the RDW approach used for Application Problems.

Student Debrief (10 minutes)

Lesson Objective: Make number bonds through ten with a subtraction focus and apply to one-step word problems.

The Student Debrief is intended to invite reflection and active processing of the total lesson experience.

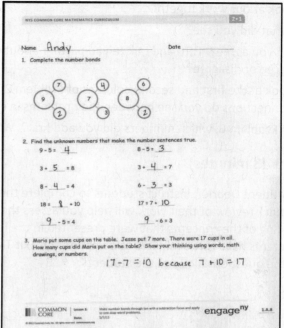

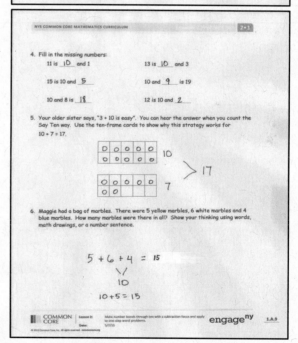

Invite students to review their solutions for the Problem Set. They should check work by comparing answers with a partner before going over answers as a class. Look for misconceptions or misunderstandings that can be addressed in the Debrief. Guide students in a conversation to debrief the Problem Set and process the lesson. You may choose to use any combination of the questions below to lead the discussion.

- You've worked hard to solve the sticker problem so now let's look at our work together.
- What did you see?
- Do you agree? Turn and talk to you partner about why you agree or disagree?
- Look at the first and second columns of Problem 2. What connections do you see between the problems in each row?
- In Problem 6, which numbers did you add first? Why?

Exit Ticket (3 minutes)

After the Student Debrief, instruct students to complete the Exit Ticket. A quick review of their work will help you assess the students' understanding of the concepts that were presented in the lesson today. Students have three minutes to complete the Exit Ticket. You may read the questions aloud to the students.

NOTES ON USING MP.3 IN A STUDENT DEBRIEF:

In transitioning from the Application Problems to the Student Debrief, anticipate your students needing one minute to organize their materials and find their pre-assigned math partner to come to the rug.

As students organize themselves, quickly project or redraw the student sample you selected, as well as your own solution on the board.

Once students have gathered, wait for 100% attention before beginning. Signal the beginning of the Debrief with a welcoming statement as modeled to the left.

The simple question, "What do you see?" is non-threatening and remarkably effective for eliciting a range of observations and insights that get the conversation started by meeting students where they are. These insights then lead to the opportunity to construct viable arguments and critique the reasoning of others.

COMMON CORE™

Lesson 2:   Make number bonds through ten with a subtraction focus and apply to one-step word problems.
Date: 6/25/13

1.A.24

Name _____   Date _____

1. Complete the number bonds

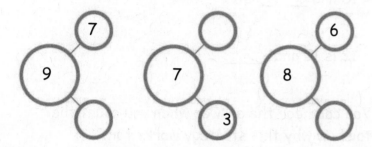

2. Find the unknown numbers that make the number sentences true.

   9 – 5 = _____   8 – 5 = _____

   3 + _____ = 8   3 + _____ = 7

   8 – _____ = 4   6 – _____ = 3

   18 = _____ + 10   17 = 7 + _____

   _____ – 5 = 4   _____ – 6 = 3

3. Maria put some cups on the table. Jesse put 7 more. There were 17 cups in all. How many cups did Maria put on the table? Show your thinking using words, math drawings, or numbers.

COMMON CORE™ | Lesson 2: | Make number bonds through ten with a subtraction focus and apply to one-step word problems.
| Date: | 6/25/13

1.A.25

4. Fill in the missing numbers:

   11 is _____ and 1   13 is _____ and 3

   15 is 10 and _____   10 and _____ is 19

   10 and 8 is _____   12 is 10 and _____

5. Your older sister says, "3 + 10 is easy". You can hear the answer when you count the Say Ten way. Use the ten-frame cards to show why this strategy works for

   10 + 7 = 17.

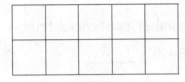

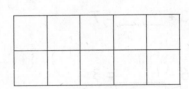

6. Maggie had a bag of marbles. There were 5 yellow marbles, 6 white marbles and 4 blue marbles. How many marbles were there in all? Show your thinking using words, math drawings, or a number sentence.

COMMON CORE™   Lesson 2:   Make number bonds through ten with a subtraction focus and apply to one-step word problems.   1.A.26

Date: 6/25/13

© 2013 Common Core, Inc. All rights reserved. commoncore.org

Name _____   Date _____

1. 7 – 4 = _____

2. 2 + _____ = 8

3. 6 = 9 – _____

4. Mr. Gardener has a box with 12 tomatoes. He gives 2 tomatoes to his sister and another 7 tomatoes to his neighbor. How many tomatoes does he have left? Show your work with a picture and number sentence.

    Mr. Gardener has _____ tomatoes.

COMMON CORE™   Lesson 2:   Make number bonds through ten with a subtraction focus and apply to one-step word problems.

Date: 6/25/13

1.A.27

Name _____   Date _____

1. Complete the number bonds

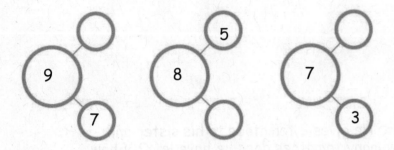

2. Find the unknown numbers that make the number sentences true.

7 – 5 = _____   9 – 5 = _____

4 + _____ = 8   10 = 7 + _____

8 – _____ = 3   7 – _____ = 3

17 = _____ + 10   6 = 5 + _____

_____ – 5 = 3   _____ – 6 = 3

3. Fill in the missing numbers
_____ = 8 + 10   _____ = 7 – 2

_____ = 10 – 5   _____ = 10 + 4

_____ = 10 + 9   _____ = 3 + 6

 **Lesson 2:**   Make number bonds through ten with a subtraction focus and apply
to one-step word problems.
Date: 6/25/13

1.A.28

4. Fill in the missing numbers.

16 is _____ and 6.

11 is 10 and _____

18 is _____ and 10

10 and 7 is _____

15 is _____ ten _____ ones.

10 and _____ is 19

5. Mr. Avakian put a stack of 10 paper plates on the table for a party. He also put 8 big plates of food. How many plates were there in all on the table? Show your thinking using words, math drawings, or a number sentence.

6. Mr. Passerini handed out 10 vanilla, 2 chocolate, and 8 strawberry ice cream cones. How many ice cream cones did she hand out in all? Show your thinking using words, math drawings, or a number sentence.

COMMON CORE™

Lesson 2:

Date:

Make number bonds through ten with a subtraction focus and apply to one-step word problems.

6/25/13

1.A.29

GRADE 2 • MODULE 1

Topic B

Mental Strategies for Addition and Subtraction Within 20

2.OA.1, 2.OA.2

Focus Standard:	2.OA.1	Use addition and subtraction within 100 to solve one- and two-step word problems involving situations of adding to, taking from, putting together, taking apart, and comparing, with unknowns in all positions, e.g., by using drawings and equations with a symbol for the unknown number to represent the problem.
	2.OA.2	Fluently add and subtract within 20 using mental strategies. By end of grade 2, know from memory all sums of two one-digit numbers.
Instructional Days:	3	
Coherence -Links from:	G1–M2	Introduction to Place Value Through Addition and Subtraction Within 20
-Links to:	G2–M4	Addition and Subtraction Within 200 with Word Problems to 100
	G3–M2	Place Value and Problem Solving with Units of Measure

Now that students have practiced their kindergarten and Grade 1 skills, they are ready to become more fluent with addition problems, such as 8 + 7 and 5 + 9, where they must cross the ten. In Lesson 3, students make use of the ten-frame structure as they complete the unit of ten and add on the leftover ones. Students proceed to pictorial and abstract representations to demonstrate their understanding of separating the ten out from the ones, as in 8 + 4 = 12 (shown at right).

In Lesson 4, students add and subtract in the ones place within the teens. This sharpens their skill of separating the ten from the ones and applying their knowledge of sums and differences to 10 to the teen numbers (e.g., 13 + 2 = (10 + 3) + 2 = 10 + (3 + 2)). In this lesson, students also remember they can use a basic fact to subtract from the ones place when there are enough ones (e.g., 5 − 3 = 2 so 15 − 3 = 12). This understanding leads directly to Lesson 5, where students make the decision to subtract from 10 when there are not enough ones (e.g., 12 − 4, 13 − 5). Students subtract from ten when they solve a variety of one-step word problem types **(2.OA.1)**. Subtraction from 10 is a strategy that a Grade 2 student uses to solve 12 − 8 and similar problems, by taking 8 from the 10 in 12. More importantly, this strategy lays the foundation for understanding place value and our unitary system. Students must determine if there are enough ones to subtract or if they must take the number from ten, thus paving the way for recomposing units when using a written method in Modules 4 and 5.

$$8 + 4 = 12$$
$$\underset{2\ \ 2}{\diagdown}$$

A Teaching Sequence Towards Mastery of Mental Strategies for Addition and Subtraction Within 20

Objective 1: Make a ten to add within 20.
(Lesson 3)

Objective 2: Make a ten to add and subtract within 20.
(Lesson 4)

Objective 3: Decompose to subtract from a ten when subtracting within 20 and apply to one-step word problems.
(Lesson 5)

Lesson 3

Objective: Make a ten to add within 20.

Suggested Lesson Structure

■ Fluency Practice   (15 minutes)
■ Concept Development   (30 minutes)
■ Application Problems   (5 minutes)
■ Student Debrief   (10 minutes)
   Total Time   **(60 minutes)**

Fluency Practice (15 minutes)

- Break Apart and Put Together by Place Value **2.OA.2** (2 minutes)
- Take Out a Part: Numbers Within 10 **2.OA.2**   (2 minutes)
- Pairs to Make 10 with Number Sentences **2.OA.2**   (2 minutes)
- One More, Ten More **2.OA.2**   (9 minutes)

Break Apart and Put Together by Place Value (2 minutes)

Note: Students remember the relevance of their ten plus facts to larger numbers.

    T: Let's play some number games! I say 10 + 5, you say 15. Ready?
    T: 10 + 5.
    S: 15.
    T: 10 + 2.
    S: 12.

Continue with the following possible sequence: 10 + 9, 10 + 4, 20 + 4, 50 + 4, 30 + 8, and 70 + 8.

    T: How are 10 + 4 and 50 + 4 the same? How are they different?
    T: How is knowing that helpful?
    S: (Students share.)
    T: Now, I say 13, you say 10 + 3.
    T: 13.
    S: 10 + 3.

Continue with the following possible sequence: 17, 11, 16, 18, 28, 78, 14, 34, and 94.

Take Out a Part: Numbers Within 10 (2 minutes)

Note: Taking out 1 prepares students for adding 9. The students make a ten, adding 9 and 6 by adding 9 and 1 and 5. Taking out 2 prepares students for adding 8. The students make a ten, adding 8 and 6 by adding 8 and 2 and 4.

> T: Let's take out 1 from each number. I say 5. You say, 1 + 4.
> T: 5. Get ready.
> S: 1 + 4.
> T: Now let's take out 2. If I say 6, you say 2 + 4.
> T: 3.
> S: 2 + 1.

Continue with possible sequence: 5, 10, 4, 7, 9, 8, 6.

Pairs to Make 10 with Number Sentences (2 minutes)

Materials: (S) Personal white boards

Note: This is a foundational skill for mastery of sums and differences to 20.

> T: I'll say a number and you write the addition sentence to make 10 on your personal white board.
> T: 5. Get ready. Show me your board.
> S: 5 + 5 = 10.
> T: 8. Get ready. Show me your board.
> S: 8 + 2 = 10.

Continue with the following possible sequence: 9, 1, 0, 10, 6, 4, 7, and 3.

> T: What pattern did you notice that helped you solve the problems?
> S: You can just switch the numbers around! → If you say 8 and the answer is 8 + 2 = 10, then I know that when you say 2 the answer will be 2 + 8 = 10. → The numbers can switch places!

Sprint: One More, Ten More (9 minutes)

Note: In order to be flexible with adding and subtracting one unit, students first work with 1 more and 10 more.

Materials: (S) One More, Ten More Sprint

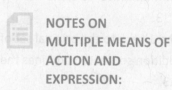

NOTES ON MULTIPLE MEANS OF ACTION AND EXPRESSION:

Some students may require extended time for Sprints:

- Create a differentiated Sprint for students whose IEPs warrant extra time by eliminating the last five problems.
- Extend time for the task based on individual student needs.
- Focus on goals for accomplishment within a time frame.
- Give students the opportunity to practice the sprint beforehand at home to help them remain calm and confident during the timed task.

Concept Development (30 minutes)

Materials: (T) Two-color counters (S) Linking cubes in two colors, personal white boards, blank paper, set of ten-frame cards for numbers 8, 9, and 10, small bag of two-color counters

Note: The focus is making 10 from a large common addend (e.g., solving 9 + 4, 9 + 5, 8 + 4, 8 + 5). Call students to the carpet and as you move the cubes, leave them as shown at right so that students can compare solutions.

T: (Present 9 counters in one set and 4 in another set directly to the right, as shown at right.)

T: How many are here (signaling the set of 9)?

S: 9.

T: How many are here (signaling the set of 4)?

S: 4.

T: (Move an object from the 4 to complete the ten.)

T: How many are here?

S: 10.

T: How many are here?

S: 3.

T: What addition sentence combines these 2 sets?

S: 10 + 3 = 13.

T: (Move the 1 back to the original set of 4.)

T: What addition sentence combines these two sets?

S: 9 + 4 = 13.

T: (Repeat the process immediately with 9 + 5.)

T: Turn and talk to your partner to compare 9 + 4 and 9 + 5. (The goal is for students to look for and make use of structure as they complete the unit of ten and add on the ones that are left over.)

T: (After the students have analyzed the problems, numerically record the make ten solutions using the number sentences and bonds shown above.)

T: On your personal white boards, draw 8 circles in a ten-frame format.

S: (Draw 8 circles.)

T: Draw 4 crosses by completing the ten first. Draw the extras to the right.

S: (Draw 4 crosses.)

T: How much more does 8 need to make ten?

S: 2 more.

T: And how many are remaining to add to ten?

S: 2.

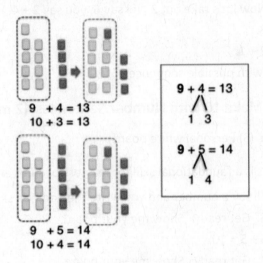

9 + 4 = 13
10 + 3 = 13

9 + 5 = 14
10 + 4 = 14

9 + 4 = 13
      /\
     1 3

9 + 5 = 14
      /\
     1 4

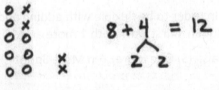

8 + 4 = 12
     /\
    2 2

T: 8 + 4 is?

S: 12.

T: 10 + 2 is?

S: 12.

T: Record the make ten solution to 8 + 4 with number bonds to show that you broke 4 into 2 and 2 to make ten.

T: (Continue with 8 + 5.)

T: Show your work to your partner and tell what you notice about adding to 8.

MP.7

T: (After students respond.) Do you remember what you noticed about adding to 9? How are 9 + 4 and 8 + 4 the same and different? Use your linking cubes or your drawing to explain.

S: You have to make 10 with both. → We used 2 to make 10 when we added to 8, and 1 to make 10 when we added to 9. → We bonded 4 as 1 and 3 and 2 and 2.

The pencil and paper work below might follow directly after students have engaged with the teacher by working on their personal white boards solving 8 + 4 and 8 + 5.

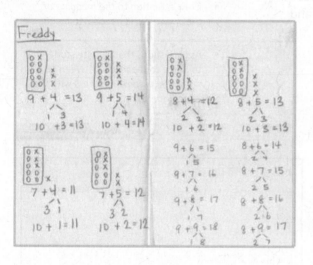

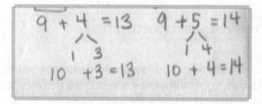

T: I don't want you to always need to draw as you solve these problems. Fold your paper so that you are only looking at the number sentences of 9 + 4 and 9 + 5. (Pause as students do so.)

T: Looking only at the number sentences, talk to your partner about the meaning of each number. What does 9 refer to as you remember the picture? 4? The bond of 1 and 3? The 13? 10 + 3?

T: Now look at your list of 9's facts. Do you notice a pattern that will help you get better at remembering these sums quickly? (The sums increase by one.)

Note: The focus in this next activity is making 10 when the smaller addend is in common. Give them lots of practice with sets of problems having a common addend, which helps them see relationships.

Directions: Pass out ten-frame cards and counters. Students model 9 + 4 and then 8 + 4 by making a ten. In the final frame of the sample sequence below, students cover 9 + 1 and 8 + 2 with a ten-frame card, clearly showing the 10 + fact within 9 + 4 and 8 + 4. Students write the equivalent statements: 9 + 4 = 10 + 3 and 8 + 4 = 10 + 2.

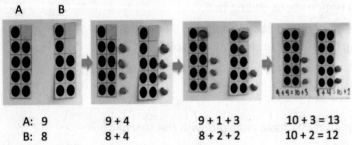

A   B

| A: 9 | 9 + 4 | 9 + 1 + 3 | 10 + 3 = 13 |
| B: 8 | 8 + 4 | 8 + 2 + 2 | 10 + 2 = 12 |

When finished with several sets of problems, students discuss with a partner how the problems within a set are the same and different.

Application Problem (5 minutes)

Ben and Chuck collect dimes. They do it by first collecting pennies and then trading with their parents 10 pennies for 1 dime. Ben has 8 pennies and Chuck has 9 pennies. They each find 4 more pennies.

- How many pennies does each boy have before they trade?
- How many extra pennies does each boy have after they trade?
- How many more pennies does each boy need before he can trade for another dime?

Note: This problem allows students to apply today's concept of make a ten to add within 20 in a real-world context. Five minutes have been allotted for this time-frame task.

Problem Set (10 minutes)

Students should do their personal best to complete the Problem Set within the allotted 10 minutes. For some classes, it may be appropriate to modify the assignment by specifying which problems they work on first. Some problems do not specify a method for solving. Students solve these problems using the RDW approach used for Application Problems.

NOTES ON MULTIPLE MEANS OF REPRESENTATION:

In this segment, students use the ten-frame model to reason about making 10 to add to the teens. Using the language of MP.2, "they pause to probe the referents" (i.e., ten-frames) "to relate them to the symbols involved" (numbers).

- Invite students to use models to calculate and explain their reasoning (e.g. 8 + 4 and 9 + 4 with linking cubes, or circles and crosses).
- Draw attention to *the meaning of the quantities* (8 needs 2 to be 10, etc.).
- Ask questions that require students to make connections between numbers (associating the 8 with the 2) and operations (e.g., 8 + _____ = 10, 10 − _____ = 8).

Ben

o x
o x
o o
o o x
o o x

8 + 4 = 10 + 2
   /\
  2 2

Chuck

o x
o o
o o x
o o x
o o x

9 + 4 = 10 + 3
   /\
  1 3

a. Ben has 12 coins. Chuck has 13 coins.

b. Ben has 2 extra pennies. Chuck has 3 extra pennies.

c. 2 + 8 = 10   Ben needs 8 more pennies.
3 + 7 = 10   Chuck needs 7 more pennies.

Student Debrief (10 minutes)

Lesson Objective: Make a ten to add within 20.

The Student Debrief is intended to invite reflection and active processing of the total lesson experience.

Invite students to review their solutions for the Problem Set. They should check work by comparing answers with a partner before going over answers as a class. Look for misconceptions or misunderstandings that can be addressed in the Debrief. Guide students in a conversation to debrief the Problem Set and process the lesson. You may choose to use any combination of the questions below to lead the discussion.

- Let's look at page one of your worksheet. How are 8 + 3 and 10 + 1 related?
- Talk to your partner about how we can explain that relationship using a drawing.
- How can you relate 19 + 5 and 20 + 4 to 9 + 5 and 10 + 4?
- What would be another set of problems to relate to 9 + 5 and 10 + 4?
- Talk to your partner about what you think is our lesson's focus today.

Exit Ticket (3 minutes)

After the Student Debrief, instruct students to complete the Exit Ticket. A review of their work will help you assess the students' understanding of the concepts that were presented in the lesson today and plan more effectively for future lessons. You may read the questions aloud to the students.

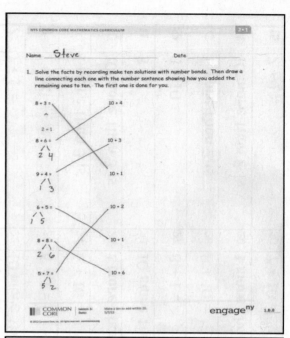

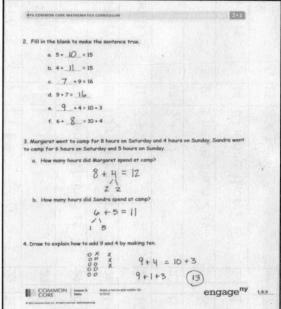

A. Do as many as you can in 60 seconds.

1	1 more than 4 is	16	2 + 10 =
2	10 more than 4 is	17	1 more than 5 is
3	4 + 1 =	18	10 more than 5 is
4	4 + 10 =	19	5 + 1 =
5	1 more than 1 is	20	5 + 10 =
6	10 more than 1 is	21	1 more than 6 is
7	1 + 1 =	22	10 more than 6 is
8	1 + 10 =	23	6 + 1 =
9	1 more than 3 is	24	6 + 10 =
10	10 more than 3 is	25	1 more than 8 is
11	3 + 1 =	26	10 more than 8 is
12	3 + 10 =	27	8 + 1 =
13	1 more than 2 is	28	8 + 10 =
14	10 more than 2 is	29	1 more than 7 is
15	2 + 1 =	30	7 + 10 =

B. Do as many as you can in 60 seconds.

1	1 more than 4 is	16	2 + 10 =
2	10 more than 4 is	17	1 more than 5 is
3	4 + 1 =	18	10 more than 5 is
4	4 + 10 =	19	5 + 1 =
5	1 more than 1 is	20	5 + 10 =
6	10 more than 1 is	21	1 more than 6 is
7	1 + 1 =	22	10 more than 6 is
8	1 + 10 =	23	6 + 1 =
9	1 more than 3 is	24	6 + 10 =
10	10 more than 3 is	25	1 more than 8 is
11	3 + 1 =	26	10 more than 8 is
12	3 + 10 =	27	8 + 1 =
13	1 more than 2 is	28	8 + 10 =
14	10 more than 2 is	29	1 more than 7 is
15	2 + 1 =	30	7 + 10 =

COMMON CORE | Lesson 3: | Make a ten to add within 20. | 1.B.9
Date: | 6/25/13

Name _____   Date _____

1. Solve the facts by recording make ten solutions with number bonds. Then draw a line connecting each one with the number sentence showing how you added the remaining ones to ten. The first one is done for you.

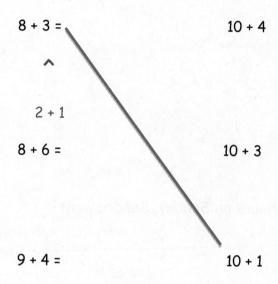

8 + 3 =   10 + 4

     2 + 1

8 + 6 =   10 + 3

9 + 4 =   10 + 1

6 + 5 =   10 + 2

8 + 8 =   10 + 1

5 + 7 =   10 + 6

2. Fill in the blank to make the sentence true.

    a. $5 + \underline{\hspace{1cm}} = 15$

    b. $4 + \underline{\hspace{1cm}} = 15$

    c. $\underline{\hspace{1cm}} + 9 = 16$

    d. $9 + 7 = \underline{\hspace{1cm}}$

    e. $\underline{\hspace{1cm}} + 4 = 10 + 3$

    f. $6 + \underline{\hspace{1cm}} = 10 + 4$

3. Margaret went to camp for 8 hours on Saturday and 4 hours on Sunday. Sandra went to camp for 6 hours on Saturday and 5 hours on Sunday.

   a. How many hours did Margaret spend at camp?

   b. How many hours did Sandra spend at camp?

4. Draw to explain how to add 9 and 4 by making ten.

Name _____   Date _____

1. Draw to explain 8 + 6 = 10 + 4.

2. Solve.

    a. 9 + 7 = _____ + 6

    b. _____ + 3 = 10 + 2

    c. 7 + _____ = 10 + 1

Name _____   Date _____

1. Solve the facts by recording make ten solutions with number bonds. Then draw a line connecting each one with the number sentence showing how you added the remaining ones to ten. The first one is done for you.

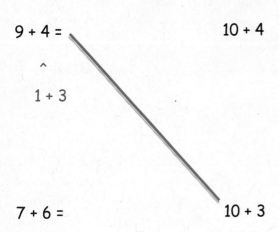

9 + 4 =   10 + 4

  ^

  1 + 3

7 + 6 =   10 + 3

6 + 6 =   10 + 3

7 + 9 =   10 + 2

6 + 8 =   10 + 6

7 + 7 =   10 + 4

2. Jennifer has 9 markers at school and 6 at home. Orlando has 7 markers at school and 8 at home.
   a. How many markers does Jennifer have?

   b. How many markers does Orlando have?

3. Fill in the blank to make the sentence true.
   a. 9 + 5 = _____ + 4

   b. 4 + 8 = 10 + _____

   c. 8 + _____ = 10 + 5

   d. _____ + 5 = 10 + 2

4. Two teams are playing a baseball game. Team Tigers has 9 players on the field and 4 players on the bench. Team Lion has 9 players on the field and 7 players on the bench.
   a. How many players does Team Tiger have?

   b. How many players does Team Lion have?

5. Draw to explain how to add 7 and 6 by making ten.

Lesson 4

Objective: Make a ten to add and subtract within 20.

Suggested Lesson Structure

■ Fluency Practice	(15 minutes)
■ Concept Development	(20 minutes)
■ Application Problems	(15 minutes)
■ Student Debrief	(10 minutes)
Total Time	**(60 minutes)**

Fluency Practice (15 minutes)

- Take from 10 **2.OA.2**   (5 minutes)
- Make a Ten to Add **2.OA.2**   (6 minutes)
- Say Ten Counting from 25 to 9 **2.NBT.1** (4 minutes)

Take from 10 (5 minutes)

Materials: (S) Personal white boards

Note: *Take from 10* develops the automaticity necessary to subtract fluently from the ten when subtracting from the teens.

T: Let's play Take from 10! When I say one, you say nine because the game is to take the number I say from 10. Ready? 2.

S: 8.

Continue with the following sequence: 3, 6, 5, 9.

T: This time, after you say how many are left, write the number sentence on your personal white board. Wait for my signal to show it.   5.

S: 5.

S: (Write the number sentence on their boards.)

T: (Signal.)

S: (Students show 10 – 5 = 5.)

Continue with the following possible sequence: 7, 8, 6, 9, and 4.

> **NOTES ON MULTIPLE MEANS OF ENGAGEMENT:**
>
> Support oral responses for Make a Ten to Add by providing personal white boards and ten-frames to students as needed. Draw a ten-frame on the board so students can visualize the ten being made.
>
>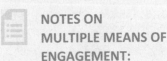
>
> X
>
> 9 + 2 = 10 + 1

Lesson 4:   Make a ten to add and subtract within 20.
Date: 6/25/13

1.B.15

Make a Ten to Add (6 minutes)

Note: Reviewing making ten allows us in this lesson to then add within the teens during the lesson and see the distinction.

T: Let's make ten to add. I say 9 + 2, and you say 9 + 2 = 10 + 1. Ready? 9 + 2.

S: 9 + 2 = 10 + 1.

T: Answer?

S: 11.

T: 9 + 5.

S: 9 + 5 = 10 + 4

T: Answer?

S: 14.

Continue with the following possible sequence: 9 + 7; 9 + 6; 9 + 8; 8 + 3; 8 + 7; 7 + 4; and 7 + 6.

Say Ten Counting from 25 to 9 (4 minutes)

Materials: (S) Hide Zero cards, Rekenrek

Note: Today's lesson involves using basic sums and differences within ten to solve problems within the teens that do not cross the ten. This relies on a solid grasp of the structure of ten.

T: (Show 12 with Hide Zero cards.) 2 more than 10, not in Say Ten way?

S: 12

T: (Pull cards apart.) The Say Ten way is to say 12?

S: 1 ten 2

T: (Show 13.) What is the Say Ten way for 13?

S: 1 ten 3

T: (Pull cards apart.) That's right!

T: Let's count the Say Ten way starting from 25 on the Rekenrek. As I move the beads, count aloud. What is the Say Ten way for 25?

S: 2 tens 5.

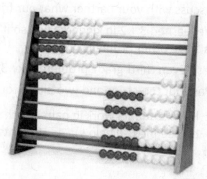

Show 25 with beads pulled to the left on the Rekenrek.

S: 2 tens 5, 2 tens 4, 2 tens 3, 2 tens 2, 2 tens 1, 2 tens, 1 ten 9, 1 ten 8, 1 ten 7, 1 ten 6, 1 ten 5, 1 ten 4, 1 ten 3, 1 ten 2, 1 ten 1, 1 ten , 9.

Concept Development (20 minutes)

Materials: (T) Two-sided counters and a ten-frame card showing 10 (S) Ten-strip and two-sided counters per student

Note: The focus of this activity is adding within the teens.

Present three objects in one set and two in another directly to the right.

T: What addition sentence combines these two sets?

S: 3 + 2 = 5.

Place a ten-frame card next to the three ones.

T: What is 10 + 3 + 2?

S: 15.

T: What is 13 + 2?

S: 15.

T: (Move the ten-frame card next to the 2.) What is 3 + 10 + 2?

S: 15.

T: What is 3 + 12?

S: 15.

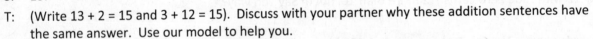

$$13 + 2 = 15$$
$$10 \quad 3$$

$$3 + 12 = 15$$
$$2 \quad 10$$

T: (Write 13 + 2 = 15 and 3 + 12 = 15). Discuss with your partner why these addition sentences have the same answer. Use our model to help you.

S: Both are equal to 10 + 5. → Both used the same basic fact in the ones, 3 + 2 = 5.

T: Discuss with your partner what our friend might mean by *basic fact*.

S: We learned 3 + 2 in kindergarten so it's basic. We already know how to do it. → Yeah, but it helps us solve other problems.

T: Yes! Even third-grade problems like 3 sevenths + 2 sevenths! Or, 3 million + 2 million.

T: (Pass out ten-strips and two-sided counters.)

Directions: Have students work in pairs. Both show 7 + 3. Then Partner A models 13 + 7 and Partner B models 7 + 13 (see picture below). As students recognize that the ones equal 10, move on to paper and pencil work.

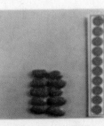

7 + 3 = 10   17 + 3 = 20   7 + 13 = 20   10 + 10 = 20

T: Talk with your partner and compare 13 + 7 = 20 and 17 + 3 = 20. (Pause while students discuss.)

T: Write at least one set of similar problems.

Circulate and choose two students' work, one which completes the ten and one which does not but does show the associative and commutative properties.

MP.3

S: 12 + 8 and 18 + 2. → 12 + 4 = 16 and 14 + 12 = 26.

T: (Recording on board.) Excellent choices.

S: But the second doesn't use a basic fact that equals ten!

T: Charles, can you defend your response?

C: I think it is the same because both problems show the switch around in the ones place.

S: Yeah, both pairs use one basic fact.

S: The teacher didn't say exactly what had to be the same. Charles just left out the *make ten*.

T: Is he wrong or right? Discuss it with your partner.

Note: The focus of this activity is subtracting within the teens.

Present five objects in one column, as pictured to the right.

T: What subtraction sentence takes away this set (cover 3 red)?

S: 5 – 3 = 2.

T: (Place a ten-frame card next to the five objects.)

T: What is 10 + 5 – 3? Subtract 3 from 5 first because there are enough ones in the ones place!

T: 5 – 3 is?

S: 2.

T: 10 + 2 is?

S: 12.

T: What is 15 – 3?

S: 12.

T: (Write 10 + 2 = 12 and 15 – 3 = 12). Show using a picture why these number sentences have the same answer.

S: The 2 is what is left after you take away 3 ones from 5 ones. → Cover up the tens. It says 5 – 3 is 2. Then just add the ten again. → It's using a basic fact.

T: We can take 3 from the ones because there are enough ones. What if we had 15 – 6? Do we have enough ones then?

S: No!

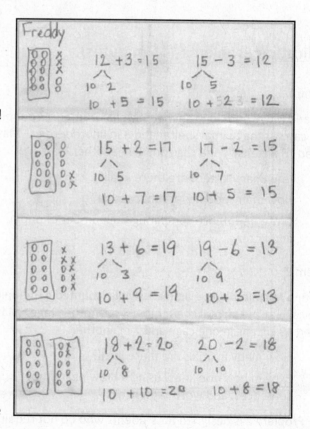

T: With your partner, come up with at least two examples where there are not enough ones to subtract from the ones.

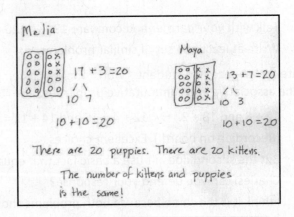

In this final activity (pictured above), the two concepts of addition and subtraction come together using a part–whole model to represent related facts. (Teacher models a few number bonds as shown in the problem set to the right).

Directions: Students model and write a related pair of addition and subtraction problems where there are enough ones in the ones place to subtract from the ones. Students may begin with the problems 12 + 3 = 15 and 15 – 3 = 12. Circulate and ask, "What basic addition fact is related to 12 + 3 = 15?"

As an extension, students may model and write at least two other related pairs of addition and subtraction problems where there are enough ones in the ones place to subtract from the ones.

Application Problems (15 minutes)

Problem 1

Melia and Maya both love animals. Melia counted 17 puppies in one cage at the animal shelter and 3 in another cage. Maya counted 13 kittens in one cage and 7 in another.

- How many kittens are there in all?
- How many puppies are there in all?
- Write a sentence comparing the number of puppies and kittens.

Problem 2

Melia and Maya both love animals. Melia counted 47 puppies in one cage at the animal shelter and 3 in another cage. Maya counted 43 kittens in one cage and 7 in another.

- How many animals are there in all?
- Explain how you know using a drawing, number sentences, and word sentences.

Note: Problem 2 is designed for students who do not require guided practice. Both problems are an application of today's lesson, in which students added the basic facts in the ones place to add within 20.

NOTES ON APPLICATIONS:

These are the four steps of the problem-solving process:

1. Read
2. Draw
3. Write a sentence
4. Write a word sentence

This process provides accommodation for SWD and ELL students since it is both visual and kinesthetic. The exemplar of MP.2 to the left is a guided process, which also certainly supports the same subgroups.

To accommodate for advanced students who may be bored by this pace, you might give them Problem 2 instead of engaging them in guided practice for Problems 1.

NOTES ON MULTIPLE MEANS OF REPRESENTATION:

During the Debrief, students use personal white boards to write related problems. Accelerated learners can be challenged to write as many problems in a time frame. Give these students a purpose by placing extra problems in a bonus box to be used for future homework assignments, with credit given to the author.

The intention of this lesson is for students to use number bonds and arrive at 10 + 3 + 7 = 10 + 10 and 10 + 7 + 3 = 10 + 10. Help them notice the commutative property in these equations, since the previous day's lesson focused on the associative property.

To demonstrate the commutative property, call on 3 students to stand in a line. Have them switch positions and elicit from students that no matter what position they are in, they are still the same 3 students.

Problem Set (10 minutes)

Students should do their personal best to complete the Problem Set within the allotted 10 minutes. For some classes, it may be appropriate to modify the assignment by specifying which problems they work on first. Some problems do not specify a method for solving. Students solve these problems using the RDW approach used for Application Problems.

In this Problem Set, we suggest all students begin with 1–7 and then move on to items 16–18. Possibly leave 8–15 to the end if there is still time.

Student Debrief (10 minutes)

Lesson Objective: Make a ten to add and subtract within 20.

The Student Debrief is intended to invite reflection and active processing of the total lesson experience.

Invite students to review their solutions for the Problem Set. They should check work by comparing answers with a partner before going over answers as a class. Look for misconceptions or misunderstandings that can be addressed in the Debrief. Guide students in a conversation to debrief the Problem Set and process the lesson. You may choose to use any combination of the questions below to lead the discussion.

- Talk to your partner and write a problem related to 17 + 3 on your personal board.

- Talk to your partner and write a problem related to 16 − 2 on your personal board.

- Look at the first page of the Problem Set. Talk to your partner about any connections you notice between the problems.

- Talk to your partner about what you think is our lesson's focus today.

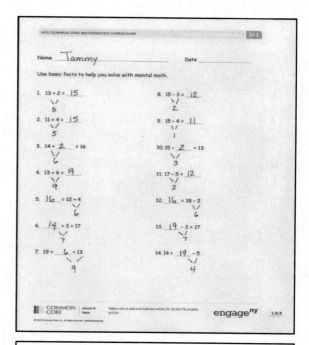

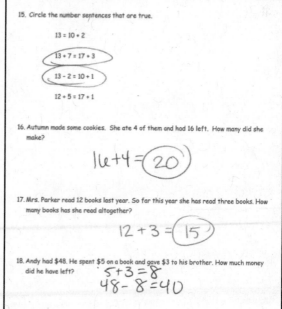

Exit Ticket (3 minutes)

After the Student Debrief, instruct students to complete the Exit Ticket. A review of their work will help you assess the students' understanding of the concepts that were presented in the lesson today and plan more effectively for future lessons. You may read the questions aloud to the students.

Name _____   Date _____

Use basic facts to help you solve with mental math.

1. 13 + 2 = _____

8. 15 – 3 = _____

2. 11 + 4 = _____

9. 15 – 4 = _____

3. 14 + _____ = 16

10. 15 – _____ = 13

4. 13 + 6 = _____

11. 17 – 5 = _____

5. _____ = 12 + 4

12. _____ = 18 – 2

6. _____ + 3 = 17

13. _____ – 2 = 17

7. 19 = _____ + 13

14. 14 = _____ – 5

15. Circle the number sentences that are true.

    $13 = 10 + 2$

    $13 + 7 = 17 + 3$

    $13 - 2 = 10 + 1$

    $12 + 5 = 17 + 1$

16. Autumn made some cookies. She ate 4 of them and had 16 left. How many did she make?

17. Mrs. Parker read 12 books last year. So far this year she has read three books. How many books has she read altogether?

18. Andy had $48. He spent $5 on a book and gave $3 to his brother. How much money did he have left?

Name _____   Date _____

Solve the problems. Write the basic fact that helps you solve each one. The first one is done for you.

1. 14 – 1 = **13**
    Basic Fact: **4 – 1 = 3**

2. 14 + 1 = _____
    Basic Fact: _____

3. 15 + 3 = _____
    Basic Fact: _____

4. 18 + 2 = _____
    Basic Fact: _____

5. 17 – 6 = _____
    Basic Fact: _____

6. 19 + 7 = _____
    Basic Fact: _____

7. 16 + 4 = _____
    Basic Fact: _____

8. 12 + 8 = _____
    Basic Fact: _____

Name _____   Date _____

Use basic facts to help you solve with mental math.

1. 16 + 3 = _____   2. 13 – 6 = _____

3. 4 + 15 = _____   4. 14 + 5 = _____

5. 7 + 11 = _____   6. 17 + 1 = _____

7. 17 + 3 = _____   8. 13 + 7 = _____

9. 14 – 4 = _____   10. 18 – 8 = _____

11. 19 – 3 = _____   12. 18 – 4 = _____

13. 16 – 3 = _____   14. 17 – 5 = _____

15. Circle the number sentences that are true.

    17 = 12 + 5

    14 + 4 = 13 + 3

    11 – 7 = 17 + 1

    12 + 5 = 15 + 2

16. Vinny caught 12 baseballs during the first game of the day. He caught some more during the second game of the day. If he caught 19 baseballs during both games, how many baseballs did he catch in the second game?

17. Draw ten-frame cards to explain why 14 + 2 = 12 + 4.

Lesson 5

Objective: Decompose to subtract from a ten when subtracting within 20 and apply to one-step word problems.

Suggested Lesson Structure

■ Fluency Practice   (7 minutes)
■ Concept Development   (26 minutes)
■ Application Problems   (17 minutes)
■ Student Debrief   (10 minutes)
   Total Time   **(60 minutes)**

Fluency Practice (7 minutes)

- Take from 10 **2.OA.2**   (3 minutes)
- Take from the Ones **2.OA.2**   (4 minutes)

Take from 10 (3 minutes)

Note: This allows for fluency when subtracting from ten when the subtrahend is greater than the ones digit.

  T: Let's play Take from 10! When I say 1, you say 9. $10 - 1 = 9$. Ready? 2.
  S: 8.
  T: Number sentence.
  S: $10 - 2 = 8$.

Continue with the following sequence: 7, 4, 9, 0, 5, 8.

Take from the Ones (4 minutes)

Note: As students realize that at times they have enough ones to subtract, they then become aware that sometimes they do not and must take from the ten.

  T: Let's take from the ones. $5 - 3 =$ _____.
  S: 2.
  T: $15 - 3 =$ _____.
  S: 12.

NOTES ON MULTIPLE MEANS OF ENGAGEMENT:

Provide students with a 20-bead Rekenrek, so they can see numbers to 10 as a number line on one row or a ten-frame (5 beads on two rows). You may also connect numbers to concrete experiences by encouraging ELLs to show their answers with their fingers.

COMMON CORE™   Lesson 5:   Decompose to subtract from a ten when subtracting within 20 and apply to one-step word problems.   1.B.27
Date: 6/25/13

© 2013 Common Core, Inc. All rights reserved. **commoncore.org**

Continue with the following possible sequence: $6 - 2$; $16 - 2$; $8 - 4$; $18 - 4$; $4 - 2$; $14 - 2$; $7 - 5$; $17 - 5$; $9 - 6$; $19 - 6$; $7 - 3$; $17 - 3$; $8 - 5$; $18 - 5$; $9 - 5$; $19 - 5$; $9 - 2$; and $19 - 2$.

Concept Development (26 minutes)

Materials: (T) Two-color counters (S) Personal white board, a ten-strip, a small bag of two-sided counters, and a subtracting strip (this is simply a white strip of paper, pictured in the photograph below)

Note: The focus of this activity is on solving problems with a common subtrahend (e.g., $11 - 8$, $12 - 8$, $13 - 8$, etc.).

T: (Present ten objects, eight of one color, two of another.)

T: How many objects are here (signaling the 10 arranged as 2 fives)?

S: 10.

T: If I subtract the red objects, what is left?

S: 2.

T: What subtraction sentence takes away 8?

S: $10 - 8 = 2$.

T: (Place one yellow object next to the ten.) Let's subtract 8 again.

T: How many objects are left (point to the 2 and 1)?

T: What addition sentence puts these two sets together?

S: $2 + 1 = 3$.

T: $11 - 8 = 2 + 1$?

S: Yes.

T: What subtraction sentence have we modeled?

S: $11 - 8 = 3$.

T: (Place another yellow object next to the ten.) What subtraction sentence takes away 8?

S: $12 - 8 = 4$.

T: What addition sentence puts the remaining sets together?

S: $2 + 2 = 4$.

T: $12 - 8 = 2 + 2$?

T: Explain $11 - 8 = 2 + 1$ and $12 - 8 = 2 + 2$ to your partner. Use the models to help you.

$$12 - 8 = 4$$
$$2 + 2 = 4$$

Next, students determine whether to subtract from the ten or the ones. At the concrete level, they might arrange their beans to show 14 as modeled on this page with subtracting strips.

T: $14 - 3$. Do I have enough ones to subtract 3 from the ones?

S: Yes.

COMMON CORE™

Lesson 5:   Decompose to subtract from a ten when subtracting within 20 and apply to one-step word problems.

Date: 6/25/13

1.B.28

T: Subtract 3 from 4. 14 – 3 is? (Cover 3 with subtracting strip as pictured below.)

S: 11.

T: Use addition to put together the two parts.

S: 10 + 1 = 11.

T: 14 – 8. Do I have enough ones to subtract 8 from the ones?

S: No.

T: Subtract 8 from the ten. 14 – 8 is? (Cover 8 with subtracting strip as pictured to the right.)

S: 6.

T: Use addition to put together the two parts.

S: 2 + 4 = 6.

T: 14 – 3 we subtracted from the ones. 14 – 8 we subtracted from the?

S: Ten.

T: Show me the number 13 with your ten and ones counters. (Students show a column of 10 and a column of 3 to its right.)

T: 13 – 8. Use your subtraction strip to subtract from either the ten or the ones.

T: The full number sentence is?

S: 13 – 8 = 5.

T: Did you subtract from the ten or the ones?

S: The ten.

T: Let's do another. 15 – 2. (Students show 10 and 5, and then cover 2 of the 5 ones.)

T: The full number sentence is?

S: 15 – 2 = 13.

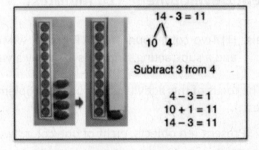

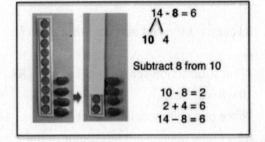

Quickly continue with other examples alternating between taking from the ones and taking 8 from the ten and asking them from which they subtracted, the ten or the ones. Using personal white boards, students record solutions with number bonds. If they still need the models, give them a ten-strip and beans with which to work.

    T: Talk to your partner. How does 10 – 9 help you to solve 13 – 9?

    T: How does 10 – 8 help you to solve 12 – 8?

Note: Just as in the previous lessons, the goal is for students to achieve fluency over time by recognizing connections and developing mental strategies that support their mastery of standard 2.OA.2. In addition to subtracting from 10 with a common minuend and subtracting from 10 with a common difference, it is also imperative that students have significant amounts of mixed practice as the year progresses.

The problems below are modeled for use in fluency activities throughout the year as you develop fluency with sums and differences to 20, with an emphasis on using 10.

Lesson 5:   Decompose to subtract from a ten when subtracting within 20 and
             apply to one-step word problems.

Date: 6/25/13

1.B.29

If there is time within today's lesson, you may advance to these problems.

Subtract from 10 with a common minuend.

11 – 2; 11 – 3; 11 – 4; 11 – 5; 11 – 6; 11 – 7; 11 – 8; 11 – 9.

12 – 3; 12 – 4; 12 – 5; 12 – 6; 12 – 7; 12 – 8; 12 – 9.

13 – 4; 13 – 5; 13 – 6; 13 – 7; 13 – 8; 13 – 9.

14 – 5; 14 – 6; 14 – 7; 14 – 8; 14 – 9.

15 – 6; 15 – 7; 15 – 8; 15 – 9.

16 – 7; 16 – 8; 16 – 9.

17 – 8; 17 – 9.

18 – 9.

Subtract from 10 with a common difference. Over time, present students with opportunities to realize that when subtracting from 12, for example, we always are adding back the 2 ones.

11 – 2; 12 – 3; 13 – 4; 14 – 5; 15 – 6; 16 – 7; 17 – 8; 18 – 9.

11 – 3; 12 – 4; 13 – 5; 14 – 6; 15 – 7; 16 – 8; 17 – 9.

11 – 4; 12 – 5; 13 – 6; 14 – 7; 15 – 8; 16 – 9.

11 – 5; 12 – 6; 13 – 7; 14 – 8; 15 – 9.

11 – 6; 12 – 7; 13 – 8; 14 – 9.

NOTES ON PACING:

The work thus far takes the entire 26 minutes. Concept 2 and Concept 3 problems are modeled for use in fluency activities throughout the year as you develop fluency with sums and differences to 20, with an emphasis on using 10. If there is time within the day's lesson, you may want to advance to Concept 2 and Concept 3 problems.

There are clearly other strategies for subtracting from the teens such as counting back and adding on. However, the "take from ten" strategy develops the important skill of breaking apart a unit relevant to work with place value, measurement, units, and fractions.

Application Problems (17 minutes)

Problem 1

Pencils come 12 to a package. Shane gives some pencils to his friends. Now he has 7 left. How many pencils did he give away?

Problem 2

Sylvia has a dime and three pennies. A friend asked her for 8 cents.

- What can Sylvia do to be able to give her friend 8 cents?
- How much money would she have left after giving away 8 cents?

MP.1

COMMON CORE™

Lesson 5:   Decompose to subtract from a ten when subtracting within 20 and apply to one-step word problems.

Date: 6/25/13

1.B.30

Note: Today's problems provide practice decomposing to subtract from a ten. Some students may simply know the answer, so it is important to establish the purpose of the application portion of each lesson. It is the time to focus on understanding the situation presented in the problem and representing that situation with a drawing and an equation. It is also the time for students to share their representations and their ways of thinking, which can help more students access problem-solving strategies. Below is a sample script to guide students through Problem 2.

MP.1

S: (Students read chorally.)

T: (Model one dime and three pennies.) Count the value of the money. At the signal tell me your answer. (Signal.)

S: 13!

T: 13 what? Remember to always state the unit.

S: 13 cents!

T: Talk to your partner about how Sylvia can give her friend 8 cents.

S: She can't. → Yeah, she can, she has 13 cents and 13 is more than 8. → We can switch a dime for ten pennies. → Oh, yeah, then there are enough pennies to give 8.

Listen as you circulate and provide advancing questions to move students forward on this continuum. At times you might want to speak very quietly, and at other times you might want to speak loudly enough that the whole class has access to the hint.

T: As I moved around the room I heard lots of students suggesting that Sylvia could trade her dime for ten pennies. Thumbs up if this was your idea.

T: (Teacher models the exchange, laying them out in a ten-frame format.) Look at the model. To give her friend 8 cents, should Sylvia take the money from the ten pennies or from the three pennies? Put the answer in your mind and wait for the signal. (Signal.)

S: The ten!

T: (Cover the 10.) Can I take 8 from 3?

S: No!

T: (Cover the 3.) Can I take 8 from 10?

S: Yes!

T: Yes, because you have enough.

T: Imagine Sylvia gives her friend the eight pennies. Turn and talk to your partner about how many pennies are left in all. (Pause.) At the signal tell me how many. (Signal.)

S: 5!

T: (Take the eight pennies away from ten.) How many were left from the dime? (Pause.) Wait for the signal. (Signal.)

S: 2!

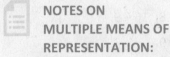

NOTES ON MULTIPLE MEANS OF REPRESENTATION:

Since the Problem Set does not include the pictorial or concrete, invite tactile learners to use their beans and subtraction strips to model the problems.

The goal in both making a 10 and taking from 10 is for students to master mental math. An important bridge is visualization. Have them use a ten-frame card, but flip it over so they cannot see the units. Allow students to peek if they must, but encourage them to visualize the quantity next time.

Lesson 5:   Decompose to subtract from a ten when subtracting within 20 and apply to one-step word problems.

Date: 6/25/13

MP.1

T: How many were left from the extra pennies? (Isolate the set with your hands.)

S: 3!

T: What addition sentence combines these?

S: 2 + 3 = 5!

T: (Write the number sentence 13 − 8 = 2 + 3). Turn and talk to your partner about what each number means in this number sentence.

Problem Set (10 minutes)

Students should do their personal best to complete the Problem Set within the allotted 10 minutes. For some classes, it may be appropriate to modify the assignment by specifying which problems they work on first. Some problems do not specify a method for solving. Students solve these problems using the RDW approach used for Application Problems.

On this Problem Set, we suggest all students begin with the first column on page 1, then move on to item 4. Possibly leave the remaining columns of problems and items 2 and 3 to the end if they still have time.

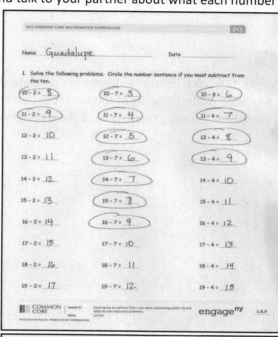

Student Debrief (10 minutes)

Lesson Objective: Decompose to subtract from a ten when subtracting within 20 and apply to one-step word problems.

The Student Debrief is intended to invite reflection and active processing of the total lesson experience.

Invite students to review their solutions for the Problem Set. They should check work by comparing answers with a partner before going over answers as a class. Look for misconceptions or misunderstandings that can be addressed in the Debrief. Guide students in a conversation to debrief the Problem Set and process the lesson. You may choose to use any combination of the questions below to lead the discussion.

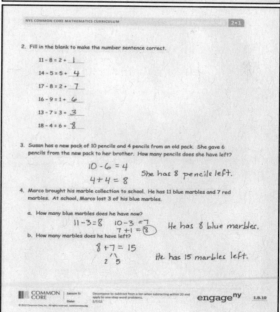

COMMON CORE™ | Lesson 5:
Date:

Decompose to subtract from a ten when subtracting within 20 and apply to one-step word problems.
6/25/13

1.B.32

© 2013 Common Core, Inc. All rights reserved. commoncore.org

- Let's look at the first column on the Problem Set. How does knowing 10 – 2 help me solve the rest of the problems?
- What is the relationship of the problems in Column 2?
- What basic fact helps me solve the problems in Column 2? Column 3?
- In number 2, 11 – 8 = 2 + _____, where did the 2 come from?

Exit Ticket

After the Student Debrief, instruct students to complete the Exit Ticket. A review of their work will help you assess the students' understanding of the concepts that were presented in the lesson today and plan more effectively for future lessons. You may read the questions aloud to the student.

Lesson 5:   Decompose to subtract from a ten when subtracting within 20 and
             apply to one-step word problems.
Date: 6/25/13

1.B.33

© 2013 Common Core, Inc. All rights reserved. commoncore.org

Name _____   Date _____

1. Solve the following problems. Circle the number sentence if you must subtract from the ten.

10 – 2 = _____   10 – 7 = _____   10 – 4 = _____

11 – 2 = _____   11 – 7 = _____   11 – 4 = _____

12 – 2 = _____   12 – 7 = _____   12 – 4 = _____

13 – 2 = _____   13 – 7 = _____   13 – 4 = _____

14 – 2 = _____   14 – 7 = _____   14 – 4 = _____

15 – 2 = _____   15 – 7 = _____   15 – 4 = _____

16 – 2 = _____   16 – 7 = _____   16 – 4 = _____

17 – 2 = _____   17 – 7 = _____   17 – 4 = _____

18 – 2 = _____   18 – 7 = _____   18 – 4 = _____

19 – 2 = _____   19 – 7 = _____   19 – 4 = _____

COMMON CORE™   Lesson 5:   Decompose to subtract from a ten when subtracting within 20 and
                    Date: apply to one-step word problems.
                                6/25/13   1.B.34

© 2013 Common Core, Inc. All rights reserved. commoncore.org

2. Fill in the blank to make the number sentence correct.

$11 - 8 = 2 + $ _____

$14 - 5 = 5 + $ _____

$17 - 8 = 2 + $ _____

$16 - 9 = 1 + $ _____

$13 - 7 = 3 + $ _____

$18 - 4 = 6 + $ _____

3. Susan has a new pack of 10 pencils and 4 pencils from an old pack. She gave 6 pencils from the new pack to her brother. How many pencils does she have left?

4. Marco brought his marble collection to school. He has 11 blue marbles and 7 red marbles. At school, Marco lost 3 of his blue marbles.

a. How many blue marbles does he have now?

b. How many marbles does he have left?

COMMON CORE™   Lesson 5:   Decompose to subtract from a ten when subtracting within 20 and apply to one-step word problems.

Date: 6/25/13   **1.B.35**

Name _____   Date _____

Complete each set.

15 – 9
/\
— —

10 – 9 = _____

1 + 5 = _____

15 – 9 = _____

14 – 6
/\
— —

10 – 6 = _____

4 + 4 = _____

14 – 6 = _____

11 – 8
/\
— —

10 – _____ = _____

_____ + 1 = _____

11 – 8 = _____

12 – 7
/\
— —

10 – _____ = _____

_____ + 2 = _____

12 – 7 = _____

Name _____   Date _____

1. Solve the following problems. Circle the number sentence if you must subtract from
   the ten.

10 – 3 = _____	10 – 5 = _____	10 – 6 = _____
11 – 3 = _____	11 – 5 = _____	11 – 6 = _____
12 – 3 = _____	12 – 5 = _____	12 – 6 = _____
13 – 3 = _____	13 – 5 = _____	13 – 6 = _____
14 – 3 = _____	14 – 5 = _____	14 – 6 = _____
15 – 3 = _____	15 – 5 = _____	15 – 6 = _____
16 – 3 = _____	16 – 5 = _____	16 – 6 = _____
17 – 3 = _____	17 – 5 = _____	17 – 6 = _____
18 – 3 = _____	18 – 5 = _____	18 – 6 = _____
19 – 3 = _____	19 – 5 = _____	19 – 6 = _____

COMMON CORE™   Lesson 5:   Decompose to subtract from a ten when subtracting within 20 and
                           apply to one-step word problems.
                  Date: 6/25/13   1.B.37

2. Fill in the blank to make the number sentence correct.

$$14 - 8 = 2 + \underline{\hspace{2cm}}$$

$$15 - 6 = 4 + \underline{\hspace{2cm}}$$

$$18 - 9 = 1 + \underline{\hspace{2cm}}$$

$$16 - 7 = 3 + \underline{\hspace{2cm}}$$

$$11 - 5 = 5 + \underline{\hspace{2cm}}$$

$$13 - 4 = 6 + \underline{\hspace{2cm}}$$

3. Mrs. Jones bought 12 eggs from the store in the morning. Her husband brought home 5 more eggs in the evening. They used 8 of the eggs for dinner. How many eggs do they have left?

4. 11 pink roses and 7 red roses grew in Mrs. Thompson's garden. She gave away 9 of the pink roses to her neighbor. How many roses does she have left?

COMMON CORE™   Lesson 5:   Decompose to subtract from a ten when subtracting within 20 and
apply to one-step word problems.   **1.B.38**
Date: 6/25/13

Topic C

Strategies for Addition and Subtraction Within 100

2.OA.1, **2.NBT.5**, 2.OA.2, 1.NBT.4, 1.NBT.5, 1.NBT.6

Focus Standard:	2.OA.1	Use addition and subtraction within 100 to solve one- and two-step word problems involving situations of adding to, taking from, putting together, taking apart, and comparing, with unknowns in all positions, e.g., by using drawings and equations with a symbol for the unknown number to represent the problem.
	2.NBT.5	Fluently add and subtract within 100 using strategies based on place value, properties of operations, and/or the relationship between addition and subtraction.
Instructional Days:	3	
Coherence -Links from:	G1–M2	Introduction to Place Value Through Addition and Subtraction Within 20
-Links to:	G2–M2	Addition and Subtraction Within of Length Units
	G2–M4	Addition and Subtraction Within 200 with Word Problems to 100

In Topic C, students revisit their addition and subtraction skills, practicing with larger numbers up to 100. Throughout this topic, students use ten-frames and number bonds to add and subtract using the structure of ten. In Lesson 6, students only add or subtract a number less than 10 without crossing the multiple (e.g., 63 + 2, 65 – 2). Students use their knowledge of basic facts and place value to solve problems with larger numbers. For example, knowing that 5 – 2 = 3 enables the student to easily subtract 65 – 2. At times, students respond using the Say Ten form (e.g., 26 is 2 tens 6) to see that in a sequence (e.g., 6 – 4, 16 -4, 26 – 4, 36 – 4, etc.) the number of tens changes but the basic fact remains the same.

Lesson 7 builds upon students' knowledge of basic facts within the teens (e.g., 7 + 8 = 15) to add 2-digit and 1-digit numbers (e.g., 77 + 8 = 85). Hence, the new complexity is to cross a multiple of 10. Students apply 7 + 5 = 10 + 2 to easily solve 87 + 5 = 90 + 2 (on right). Again, students make use of the ten structure and place value to separate a two-digit number into tens and ones, and bond smaller numbers to make a ten.

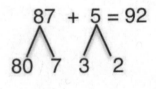

Lesson 8 mirrors the work of Lesson 7 in that students subtract single-digit numbers from multiples of 10. Students use 10 – 3 to solve 90 – 3 (on right), and they use this strategy to solve a variety of one-step word problem types. Also, since students know partners of ten with automaticity, adding some ones after taking from the ten should not be too challenging (e.g., 91

3 = 88). Topic C culminates with students learning that it is possible to "get out the ten" in problems such as 23 – 9 and add back the remaining part, such that 13 + (10 – 9) = 14. This decomposing to make or take from a ten prepares students for adding and subtracting three-digit numbers in Module 4.

A Teaching Sequence Towards Mastery of Strategies for Addition and Subtraction Within 100
Objective 1: Add and subtract within multiples of ten based on understanding place value and basic facts.   (Lesson 6)
Objective 2: Add within 100 using properties of addition to make a ten.   (Lesson 7)
Objective 3: Decompose to subtract from a ten when subtracting within 100 and apply to one-step word problems.   (Lesson 8)

Lesson 6

Objective: Add and subtract within multiples of ten based on understanding place value and basic facts.

Suggested Lesson Structure

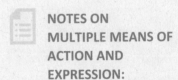

■ Fluency Practice   (20 minutes)
■ Concept Development   (30 minutes)
■ Student Debrief   (10 minutes)
   Total Time   **(60 minutes)**

Fluency Practice (20 minutes)

- Say Ten Counting from 26 to 58 **2.NBT.1**   (2 minutes)
- Take from 20 **2.OA.2**   (4 minutes)
- Basic Facts are Tools **2.OA.2**   (5 minutes)
- Adding Ones to Ones **2.OA.2**   (9 minutes)

Say Ten Counting from 26 to 58 (2 minutes)

Materials: (T) Hide Zero cards, Rekenrek.

Note: Students need a clear understanding of the *structure of ten* to be able to add and subtract within multiples of ten.

   T: (Show 22 with Hide Zero cards.) What is 2 more than 20, the regular way?

   S: 22.

   T: (Pull cards apart to show 20 + 2.) What is the Say Ten way to say 22?

   S: 2 tens 2.

   T: (Show 23.) What is the Say Ten way for 23?

   S: 2 tens 3.

   T: (Pull cards apart to show 20 + 3.) That's right!

   T: Let's count the Say Ten way starting from 26 on the Rekenrek. As I move the beads, count aloud. What is the Say Ten way for 26?

NOTES ON MULTIPLE MEANS OF ACTION AND EXPRESSION:

During fluency practice, students recall and build upon their prior knowledge of place value and basic facts from Grade 1. Design math centers that include concrete representations for students (e.g., Rekenrek, ten-frames, linking cubes). Suggestions for centers ideas include the following:

- Rekenrek: Make ten, add/subtract across ten, build numbers 11–20, etc.

- Ten-Frames: Roll dice and build the number, ten-frame flash (add or take away 1), two more/less, double it, etc.

- Linking cubes: Build a tower with two colors that shows a given total, build towers to 10 and relate quantities with number sentences, build partner towers and tell how many more/less.

Lesson 6:   Add and subtract within multiples of ten based on understanding place value and basic facts.
Date: 6/25/13

1.C.3

S: 2 tens 6.

Show 26 with beads pulled to the left on the Rekenrek.

S: 2 tens 7, 2 tens 8, 2 tens 9, 3 tens, 3 tens 1, 3 tens 2.

Continue counting to 5 tens 8.

Take from 20 (4 minutes)

Materials: (S) Personal white boards

Note: The lesson relies on a student's ability to make ten and apply it to multiples of ten. This exercise will give students familiarity with the skill prior to the concept development.

T: I say one, you say nine—you take the number I say from 10. Then write the number sentence and wait for my signal to show it.

T: 7.

S: 3. (Students write number sentence.)

T: Show your personal white boards.

S: (Show $10 - 7 = 3$.)

Continue with the following possible sequence: 8, 6, and 9.

T: This time instead of taking from 10, let's take from 20. Ready? 1.

S: 19. (Students write the number sentence.)

T: Show your personal white board.

S: (Show $20 - 1 = 19$.)

Continue with the following possible sequence: 3, 2, 5, 0, 6, 8, 7, 9.

Basic Facts are Tools (5 minutes)

Materials: (T) Rekenrek

Note: This activity prepares students for the day's concept development by emphasizing the presence of the *basic fact*. The Rekenrek provides visual support, enabling students to see the structure of ten. For example, $8 + 3$ is seen as $8 + 2 + 1$.

T: Our basic fact, or tool, is $8 + 2$. $8 + 2$ is?

S: 10.

T: $8 + 3$? (Show the numbers on the Rekenrek each time.)

S: $10 + 1$.

T: $8 + 7$ is?

S: $10 + 5$. (Continue with possible sequence: $9 + 5$, $9 + 4$, $9 + 8$.)

T: Our new basic fact, or tool, is $10 - 8$. $10 - 8$ is?

Lesson 6:   Add and subtract within multiples of ten based on understanding place value and basic facts.

Date: 6/25/13

1.C.4

S: 2.

T: 12 – 8 is? (Show the numbers on the Rekenrek each time.)

S: 2 + 2.

T: 15 – 8 is?

S: 2 + 5. (Continue with possible sequence: 12 – 9 and 15 – 9.)

Sprint: Adding Ones to Ones (9 minutes)

Materials: (S) Adding Ones to Ones Sprint

Note: The sprint applies prior knowledge of adding basic facts to larger numbers.

Concept Development (30 minutes)

Materials: (T) two-color counters, ten-frame cards for the number 10, set of ten-frame cards, linking cubes

Note: This activity focuses on adding and subtracting within a unit of 10 (e.g., 73 + 2, 75 – 2). Simple, basic facts such as 3 + 2 and 5 – 2 are helpful in solving problems with larger numbers. Students can use the say ten form of numbers (e.g., 13 is 1 ten 3, 26 is 2 tens 6,) to emphasize the presence of the basic fact. If the teacher asks a question the Say Ten way, the students should respond in kind.

T: (Show two-color counters.) 3 + 2 is?

S: 5.

T: 5 – 2 is?

S: 3.

T: (Lay down a ten-frame card.) 1 ten 3 + 2 is?

S: 1 ten 5.

T: 13 + 2 is?

S: 15.

T: 1 ten 5 – 2 is?

S: 1 ten 3.

T: 15 – 2 is?

S: 13.

T: (Lay down another ten-frame card.) 2 tens 3 + 2 is?

S: 2 tens 5.

T: 23 + 2 is?

S: 25.

T: Partner A, talk to your partner about how 3 + 2 helps you solve 23 + 2.

T: 2 tens 5 – 2 is?

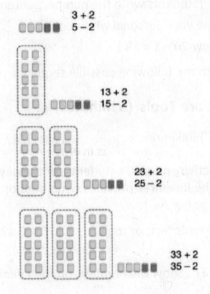

3 + 2
5 – 2

13 + 2
15 – 2

23 + 2
25 – 2

33 + 2
35 – 2

Lesson 6:   Add and subtract within multiples of ten based on understanding
             place value and basic facts.

Date: 6/25/13

1.C.5

S: 2 tens 3.

T: 25 – 2 is?

S: 23.

T: Partner B, talk to your partner about how 5 – 2 helps you solve 25 – 2.

T: (Lay down another ten-frame card.) 3 tens 3 + 2 is?

In this next activity, students will use a portion of the Problem Set to look for and make use of structure.

T: (Pass out the Problem Set.)

T: Complete numbers 1 through 8 without writing number bonds. Just write the answers. If you finish early, write more sets of problems on the back.

S: (Students work.)

T: With your partner, look at the problems with 2 + 5 and 7 – 5.

T: Partner A, read your problems aloud to Partner B the Say Ten way. Then switch.

T: Listen closely to your words. Do you hear a pattern?

S: Yes!

T: What pattern do you hear when you are adding?

S: 2 + 5.

MP.7

T: What pattern do you hear when you subtract?

S: 7 – 5.

T: Explain to your partner what is different about your problems, both in addition and subtraction.

S: The first number is different. → The 10 is different. → The number of tens is different.

T: The basic fact you heard is the same, but the number of tens changes.

T: Circle the basic fact for each set of problems and label it. Then make bonds in each of your problems to break apart the ones from the number of tens.

S: (Students work.)

T: How does 7 – 5 help you solve 67 – 5? Talk to your partner.

T: (After students share out.) Let me hear you subtract without the basic fact by counting down. Ready?

S: 66, 65, 64, 63, 62. (Anticipate that students may start at 67 and not know when to stop.)

Have students share with a partner about which strategy is easier to use, counting down or using the basic fact 7 – 5.

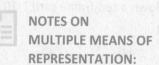

NOTES ON
MULTIPLE MEANS OF
REPRESENTATION:

In a healthy classroom culture, students may disagree with one another as they share their work. Disagreement encourages scrutiny and is an opportunity for students to learn and justify their choices. During partner talk, encourage students to justify arguments, and model and post good conversation starters: "I disagree because . . ." "Your solution is different from mine because . . ." "My error was . . ." "Your answer does not make sense to me because . . ." As you circulate, these starters should spark conversations within student partnerships.

Lesson 6:   Add and subtract within multiples of ten based on understanding place value and basic facts.

Date: 6/25/13

1.C.6

T: Think of the different numbers of tens as towers of linking cubes of different sizes. No matter what size the tower is, the 2 + 5 doesn't change. (Model this concept pictorially or concretely with linking cubes or blocks.)

T: We can use *structures* and *patterns* to make math easier. Look for structure and patterns. Here's a structure (refer to the linking cube tower). The basic fact (refer to the model of 2 + 5) helps create a number pattern when we repeatedly use it.

Now, students look for and make use of structure to extend their work in the previous segment to completing a unit of 10 with addition, e.g., 37 + 3 = 40, 87 + 3, 83 + 7. As you move through the problems modeled below, be sure to record the number sentences sequentially for reflection at the end.

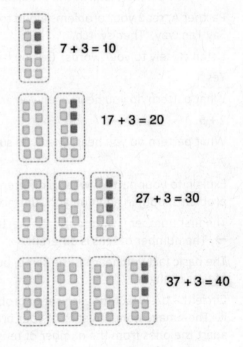

7 + 3 = 10

17 + 3 = 20

27 + 3 = 30

37 + 3 = 40

T: Present 10 counters (as shown to the right).

T: 7 + 3 is?

S: 10.

T: (Lay down a ten-frame card.) 10 + 7 + 3 is the same as?

S: 10 + 10.

T: 1 ten 7 + 3 is?

S: 2 tens.

T: 17 + 3 is? Give the addition sentence.

S: 17 + 3 = 20.

T: (Lay down a ten-frame card.) 20 + 7 + 3 is the same as?

S: 20 + 10.

T: 2 tens 7 + 3 is?

S: 3 tens.

T: 27 + 3 is? Give the addition sentence.

S: 27 + 3 = 30.

T: (Lay down a ten-frame card.) 30 + 7 + 3 is the same as?

S: 30 + 10.

T: 3 tens 7 + 3 is?

S: 4 tens.

T: 37 + 3 is? Give the addition sentence.

S: 37 + 3 = 40.

T: Let's read each equation the Say Ten way.

S: 7 + 3 = 1 ten; 1 ten 7 + 3 = 2 tens; 2 tens 7 + 3 = 3 tens; 3 tens 7 + 3 = 4 tens.

T: What pattern is repeating?

S: 7 + 3.

Lesson 6: Add and subtract within multiples of ten based on understanding place value and basic facts.

Date: 6/25/13

1.C.7

T: Let's think back to our new word *structure*. Talk to your partner about what structure 7 + 3 is standing on (point to 17 + 3 = 20). (Use this sentence frame: "7 + 3 is standing on the structure of _(1 ten) _.")

Repeat the process with each of the equations.
Depending on the time, students can generate related equations.

Problem Set (10 minutes)

Students should do their personal best to complete the Problem Set within the allotted 10 minutes. For some classes, it may be appropriate to modify the assignment by specifying which problems they work on first. Some problems do not specify a method for solving. Students solve these problems using the RDW approach used for Application Problems.

On this Problem Set, we suggest all students begin with Page 1 and then solve the word problem. Possibly leave 9–16 to the end if there is still time.

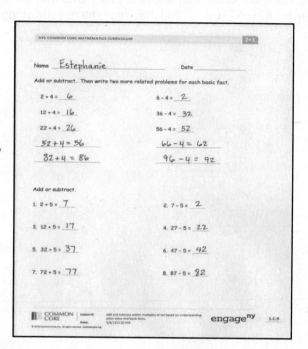

Student Debrief (10 minutes)

Lesson Objective: Add and subtract within multiples of ten based on understanding place value and basic facts.

The Student Debrief is intended to invite reflection and active processing of the total lesson experience.

Invite students to review their solutions for the Problem Set. They should check work by comparing answers with a partner before going over answers as a class. Look for misconceptions or misunderstandings that can be addressed in the Debrief. Guide students in a conversation to debrief the Problem Set and process the lesson. You may choose to use any combination of the questions below to lead the discussion.

- Look at the first section of the Problem Set. How does knowing 2 + 4 help you solve 12 + 4?

- How does solving the first column help you answer the second column?

- How do structures or patterns help make math easier?

- Talk to your partner about what you think our lesson's goal was today. Make an effort to include the word *structure* and a basic fact, using an example.

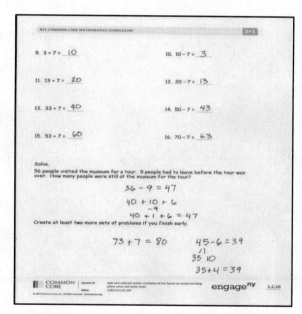

COMMON CORE™

Lesson 6:   Add and subtract within multiples of ten based on understanding
Date: place value and basic facts.
              6/25/13

1.C.8

Exit Ticket (3 minutes)

After the Student Debrief, instruct students to complete the Exit Ticket. A review of their work will help you assess the students' understanding of the concepts that were presented in the lesson today and plan more effectively for future lessons. You may read the questions aloud to the students.

Lesson 6:   Add and subtract within multiples of ten based on understanding place value and basic facts.
Date: 6/25/13

1.C.9

Do as many as you can in 60 seconds.

1	10 and 2 make	16	33 + 1 =
2	31 and 1 make	17	42 + 1 =
3	44 and 2 make	18	31 + 4 =
4	23 and 2 make	19	40 + 3 =
5	22 and 3 make	20	24 + 3 =
6	41 and 3 make	21	36 + 2 =
7	21 and 2 make	22	33 + 3 =
8	14 and 1 make	23	36 + 4 =
9	23 and 3 make	24	40 + 1 =
10	44 and 3 make	25	45 + 2 =
11	22 and 4 make	26	44 + 4 =
12	30 and 1 make	27	32 + 1 =
13	42 and 2 make	28	33 + 2 =
14	45 and 2 make	29	43 + 4 =
15	31 and 7 make	30	25 + 2 =

Can you add on the ones to the ones?

Do as many as you can in 60 seconds.

1	10 and 3 make	16	20 + 2 =
2	21 and 2 make	17	31 + 1 =
3	33 and 1 make	18	21 + 2 =
4	22 and 2 make	19	25 + 1 =
5	43 and 1 make	20	36 + 1 =
6	30 and 2 make	21	43 + 2 =
7	23 and 3 make	22	36 + 3 =
8	31 and 2 make	23	42 + 4 =
9	24 and 2 make	24	30 + 1 =
10	43 and 2 make	25	26 + 2 =
11	32 and 3 make	26	33 + 4 =
12	24 and 4 make	27	25 + 2 =
13	21 and 4 make	28	33 + 5 =
14	44 and 3 make	29	42 + 4 =
15	20 and 3 make	30	29 + 1 =

COMMON CORE

Lesson 6: Add and subtract within multiples of ten based on understanding place value and basic facts.

Date: 6/25/13

1.C.10

Name _____   Date _____

Add or subtract. Then write two more related problems for each basic fact.

2 + 4 = _____   6 – 4 = _____

12 + 4 = _____   36 – 4 = _____

22 + 4 = _____   56 – 4 = _____

_____   _____

_____   _____

Add or subtract.

1. 2 + 5 = _____   2. 7 – 5 = _____

3. 12 + 5 = _____   4. 27 – 5 = _____

5. 32 + 5 = _____   6. 47 – 5 = _____

7. 72 + 5 = _____   8. 87 – 5 = _____

COMMON CORE™ | **Lesson 6:** Add and subtract within multiples of ten based on understanding
place value and basic facts.   1.C.11
| **Date:**   6/25/13

9. 3 + 7 = _____   10. 10 - 7 = _____

11. 13 + 7 = _____   12. 20 - 7 = _____

13. 33 + 7 = _____   14. 50 - 7 = _____

15. 53 + 7 = _____   16. 70 - 7 = _____

Solve.

56 people visited the museum for a tour. 9 people had to leave before the tour was over. How many people were still at the museum for the tour?

Create at least two more sets of problems if you finish early.

Name _____   Date _____

Solve the problems. In the space provided, write a related problem for each of the basic facts.

4 + 2 =	6 – 4 =	1 + 9 =
24 + 2 =	36 – 4 =	11 + 9 =
84 + 2 =	76 – 4 =	61 + 9 =
_____	_____	_____

COMMON CORE™ | Lesson 6: | Add and subtract within multiples of ten based on understanding place value and basic facts.
| Date: | 6/25/13

1.C.13

Name _____   Date _____

Add or subtract. Then write two more related problems for each basic fact.

1. 6 + 2 = _____   2. 8 – 6 = _____

   16 + 2 = _____   28 – 6 = _____

   26 + 2 = _____   38 – 6 = _____

   _____   _____

   _____   _____

3. 4 + 3 = _____   4. 7 – 3 = _____

   44 + 3 = _____   57 – 3 = _____

   74 + 3 = _____   77 – 3 = _____

   _____   _____

   _____   _____

COMMON CORE™ | Lesson 6: | Add and subtract within multiples of ten based on understanding place value and basic facts.   1.C.14

Date: | 6/25/13

5. 5 + 2 = _____   6. 7 – 2 = _____

    35 + 2 = _____   57 – 2 = _____

    75 + 2 = _____   67 – 2 = _____

    _____   _____

    _____   _____

Solve the following 4 problems. Show your number bonds. Draw if that will help you.

1. 20 – 6 = _____   2. 30 – 5 = _____

3. 49 – 6 = _____   4. 69 – 6 = _____

Solve.

79 people attended the concert. 6 people had to leave at the break. How many people were still at the concert after the break?

COMMON CORE™ | Lesson 6:   Add and subtract within multiples of ten based on understanding
place value and basic facts.   1.C.15
Date: 6/25/13

Lesson 7

Objective: Add within 100 using properties of addition to make a ten.

Suggested Lesson Structure

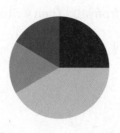

■ Fluency Practice   (15 minutes)
▨ Concept Development   (25 minutes)
▨ Application Problems   (10 minutes)
■ Student Debrief   (10 minutes)

  Total Time   **(60 minutes)**

Fluency Practice (15 minutes)

- Break Apart by Tens and Ones **2.NBT.1**   (3 minutes)
- Take from 20 **2.OA.2**   (5 minutes)
- Up to the Next Ten with Number Sentences **2.NBT.5**   (5 minutes)
- Two More **2.OA.2**   (2 minutes)

Break Apart by Tens and Ones (3 minutes)

Note: Students need to build an understanding of the place value relationship. In time, challenge students by asking "6 ones 3 tens" with students correctly replying "36".

  T: If I say 42, you say 4 tens 2 ones.
  T: If I say, 4 tens 2 ones, you say 42.
  T: 4 tens 2 ones.
  S: 42.
  T: 56.
  S: 5 tens 6 ones
  T: 7 tens 3 ones.
  S: 73

Continue with the following possible sequence: 67, 54, 49, 71, and 88.

Lesson 7:   Add within 100 using properties of addition to make a ten.
                    Date: 6/25/13

1.C.16

Take from 20 (5 minutes)

Materials: (S) Personal white boards

Note: Students use personal white boards to see the connection between taking from ten and taking from a multiple of ten.

T: I say 2, you say 8, to take the number I say from 10. Then write the number sentence and wait for my signal to show it.

T: 6.

S: 4. (Students write number sentence.)

T: Show your board.

S: (Show 10 – 6 = 4.)

Continue with the following possible sequence: 7, 9, and 5.

T: This time instead of taking from 10, let's take from 20. Ready?

T: 1.

S: 19. (Students write number sentence.)

T: Show your board.

S: (Show 20 – 1 = 19.)

Continue with the following possible sequence: 5, 6, 8, and 3.

Up to the Next Ten with Number Sentences (5 minutes)

Note: Students remember the importance of their *make ten* facts with larger numbers. By saying *up* it indicates an addition sentence.

T: If I say, "18 up," you say "2."

T: If I say, "Give me the number sentence," you say, "18 + 2 = 20." Ready?

T: 7 up.

S: 3.

T: Give me the number sentence.

S: 7 + 3 = 10.

T: 17 up.

S: 3.

T: Give me the number sentence.

S: 17 + 3 = 20.

Continue with possible sequence: 57 up, 97 up, 6 up, 4 up, 26 up, 24 up, 54 up, 74 up, 1 up, 9 up, 31 up, 61 up, and 81 up.

NOTES ON MULTIPLE MEANS OF ACTION AND EXPRESSION:

During fluency practice, provide a variety of ways for students to respond: oral; choral; student personal white boards for number sentences; concrete models (e.g., fingers, Rekenrek); pictorial models (e.g., ten-frame). Vary choral response with written response on student boards to support ELLs. Model how the use of the ten-frame can help students answer problems such as *57 up*.

| Lesson 7: | Add within 100 using properties of addition to make a ten. |
| Date: | 6/25/13 |

1.C.17

Two More (2 minutes)

Note: Students are eased into crossing multiples of ten by asking for just 2 more.

T: For every number I say, you will say what number is 2 more. If I say 2, you say 4. Ready? 3.

S: 5.

Continue with possible sequence: 6, 9, 8, 18, 38, 58, 78, 9, 19, 39, 59, and 79.

Concept Development (25 minutes)

Materials: (T) Ten-frame cards showing 10, two-color counters (S) Personal white boards

Note: This lesson focuses on addition of 2-digit and 1-digit numbers crossing multiples of 10 (e.g., 38 + 4, 47 + 6, 78 + 5, 5 + 78).

T: (Present 12 counters as shown below.)

T: 7 + 3 (Pause and point.) + 2 is?

S: 12.

T: 7 + 5 is?

S: 12.

T: (Lay down a ten-frame card.) 17 + 3 (Pause.) + 2 is?

S: 22.

T: 17 + 5 is?

S: 22.

T: 5 + 17 is?

S: 22.

T: (Lay down a ten-frame card.) 27 + 3 (Pause.) + 2 is?

S: 32.

T: 27 + 5 is? Let's read them the Say Ten way.

S: 7 + 5 = 1 ten 2. 1 ten 7 + 5 = 2 tens 2, 2 tens 7 + 5 = 3 tens 2.

T: What basic fact was used in all three problems?

S: 7 + 5 = 12.

T: On your personal white boards, work with me to solve 87 + 5 without materials. First, bond 87 as 80 and 7.

S: (Students do so.)

T: How did we bond 5 to make a ten (point to the materials)?

S: 3 and 2.

T: Excellent. 7 needs 3 to make ten. Show me that second bond.

S: (Students write the bond.)

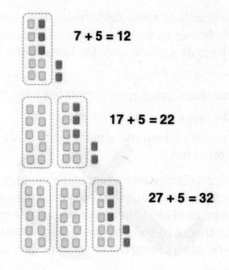

$7 + 5 = 12$

$17 + 5 = 22$

$27 + 5 = 32$

$$87 + 5 = 92$$

80 7   3   2

T: We end up with 80 + 7 + 3 + 2. Wait for the signal. Look at me when you are ready. The answer is? (Signal.)

S: 92.

T: Talk to your partner about how you know. Try using the same strategy to solve 18 + 6 on your personal board. Share if you get stuck.

Note: As students work, provide new problems as needed, varying the basic fact and increasing the number of tens for some students (e.g., 15 + 6, 45 + 6, 5 + 76, 4 + 87) while giving the same basic fact and staying under 5 tens for others who need more practice at a simpler level (e.g., 19 + 3, 29 + 3, 39 + 3). It is wise to use the personal white board rather than pencil and paper at times as students are advancing into more challenging territory. Work can quickly be erased and corrected, making error correction easy and more conducive to perseverance.

Application Problems (10 minutes)

One box fits exactly 10 cans. On Monday, Maria packed (18, 78) (see Multiple Means Note) cans into boxes, making sure to fill a box before beginning a new one. On Tuesday she added 6 more cans.

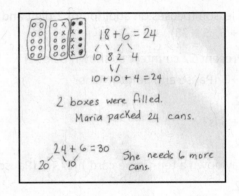

- How many boxes were completely filled then?
- How many cans did Maria pack in all?
- (Extension) How many more cans did Maria need to fill another box?

Note: In this problem, students apply the strategy they learned in today's lesson, using basic facts to bond and make a ten when crossing multiples of ten. Students who are able to work without support may choose to solve for the larger number, 78, while the teacher guides others using the smaller number, 18.

Problem Set (10 minutes)

Students should do their personal best to complete the Problem Set within the allotted 10 minutes. For some classes, it may be appropriate to modify the assignment by specifying which problems they work on first. Some problems do not specify a method for solving. Students solve these problems using the RDW approach used for Application Problems. With this Problem Set, we suggest all students begin with 1 and possibly leave 6 to the end if they still have time.

NOTES ON MULTIPLE MEANS OF ENGAGEMENT:

"(18,78)" is an invitation to choose numbers that are appropriate for different learners. Students may lack wisdom in their choice of numbers. Better to initially guide them towards the right choice for the skill set with the understanding that we are coaching them towards becoming wiser choosers.

Extension problems are always accommodations for early finishers and advanced learners.

COMMON CORE

Lesson 7:   Add within 100 using properties of addition to make a ten.
Date: 6/25/13

1.C.19

Student Debrief (10 minutes)

Lesson Objective: Add within 100 using properties of addition to make a ten.

The Student Debrief is intended to invite reflection and active processing of the total lesson experience.

Invite students to review their solutions for the Problem Set. They should check work by comparing answers with a partner before going over answers as a class. Look for misconceptions or misunderstandings that can be addressed in the Debrief. Guide students in a conversation to debrief the Problem Set and process the lesson. You may choose to use any combination of the questions below to lead the discussion.

- How does knowing 8 + 2 makes 10 help me solve 78 + 4?

- Look at numbers 1 and 2. What is the relationship between 78 + 4 and 58 + 5?

- How did the basic fact 6 + 8 help you to solve numbers 4 and 5 in the worksheet?

- How does a ten-frame model help us with learning to complete a 10 to add numbers to 100?

- Think about our story problem with the cans and the way that we solved problems with the ten-frame model. Partner B, explain to partner A how the problems are the same.

Exit Ticket (3 minutes)

After the Student Debrief, instruct students to complete the Exit Ticket. A review of their work will help you assess the students' understanding of the concepts that were presented in the lesson today and plan more effectively for future lessons. You may read the questions aloud to the students.

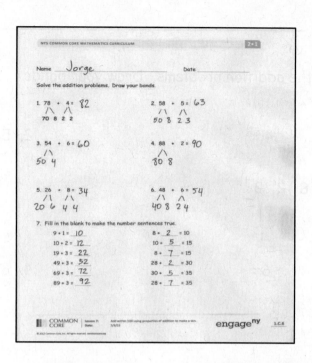

COMMON CORE™

Lesson 7:   Add within 100 using properties of addition to make a ten.
Date: 6/25/13

1.C.20

Name _____   Date _____

Solve the addition problems. Draw your bonds.

1. 78 + 4 =

   70 8 2 2

2. 58 + 5 =

3. 54 + 6 =

4. 88 + 2 =

5. 26 + 8 =

6. 48 + 6 =

7. Fill in the blank to make the number sentences true.

   9 + 1 = _____   8 + _____ = 10

   10 + 2 = _____   10 + _____ = 15

   19 + 3 = _____   8 + _____ = 15

   49 + 3 = _____   28 + _____ = 30

   69 + 3 = _____   30 + _____ = 35

   89 + 3 = _____   28 + _____ = 35

COMMON CORE™   Lesson 7:   Add within 100 using properties of addition to make a ten.
Date: 6/25/13

© 2013 Common Core, Inc. All rights reserved. commoncore.org   1.C.21

Label each number sentence as true or false.

8. 22 + 8 = 20 + 10 _____

9. 57 + 5 = 50 + 10 + 2 _____

10. 83 + 9 = 80 + 10 + 1 _____

11. 68 + 7 = 70 + 5 _____

12. 88 + 9 = 90 + 6 _____

Solve.

Jorge saved 65 dollars last month. This month he saved 8 more dollars. How much money does he have now?

Name _____   Date _____

Solve the following 4 problems. Show your number bonds. Draw if that will help you.

1. 28 + 4 = _____   2. 39 + 4 = _____
    /\   /\

3. 27 + 9 = _____   4. 38 + 9 = _____

Name _____   Date _____

Solve the addition problems. Draw your bonds.

1. 78 + 4 =   2. 58 + 5 =

   70 8 2 2

3. 36 + 6 =   4. 26 + 7 =

5. 23 + 9 =   6. 44 + 9 =

7. 47 + 8 =   8. 68 + 8 =

9. 89 + 8 =   10. 77 + 9 =

Label each number sentence as true or false.

11. 38 + 2 = 30 + 10 _____

12. 57 + 5 = 50 + 10 + 2 _____

13. 83 + 9 = 80 + 10 + 1 _____

14. 64 + 7 = 70 + 1 _____

15. 89 + 9 = 90 + 7 _____

Solve.

Anthony found 48 coins last month. This month he found 7 more coins. How many coins does he have now?

Lesson 8

Objective: Decompose to subtract from a ten when subtracting within 100 and apply to one-step word problems.

Suggested Lesson Structure

- ■ Fluency Practice   (15 minutes)
- ■ Concept Development   (20 minutes)
- ■ Application Problem   (15 minutes)
- ■ Student Debrief   (10 minutes)
- **Total Time**   **(60 minutes)**

Fluency Practice (15 minutes)

- Make a Ten **2.OA.2**   (9 minutes)
- Take from 20 **2.OA.2**   (3 minutes)
- Subtract 1 from Multiples of 10 **2.OA.2**   (3 minutes)

Sprint: Make a Ten (9 minutes)

Materials: (S) Make a Ten Sprint

Note: Students should develop automaticity to fluently make a ten when adding.

Take from 20 (3 minutes)

Materials: (S) Personal white boards

Note: Students use personal boards to see the connection between taking from ten and taking from a multiple of ten. As students show comprehension of the skill, practice verbally without the personal boards.

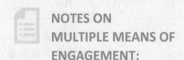

NOTES ON MULTIPLE MEANS OF ENGAGEMENT:

If this work is new to students, it may be necessary for students to use their own manipulatives to grasp the concept. Adjust the lesson times as needed. You might want to omit the sprint in order to have sufficient time for the concept development portion. Or, complete the first half of the concept development, subtracting from multiples of ten, and save the balance of the lesson for inclusion in fluency activities throughout the balance of the year.

T: I say 3, you say 7—you take the number I say from 10. Write the number sentence and wait for my signal to show it.

T: 8.

S: 2. (Students write number sentence.)

T: Show your personal boards.

Lesson 8:	Decompose to subtract from a ten when subtracting within 100 and apply to one-step word problems.
Date:	6/25/13

1.C.26

S: (Show 10 – 8 = 2.)

Continue with the following possible sequence: 4, 5, and 9.

T: This time instead of taking from 10, let's take from 20. Ready? 1.

S: 19. (Students write number sentence.)

T: Show your personal board.

S: (Show 20 – 1 = 19.)

Continue with the following possible sequence:
   3, 2, 5, 0, 6, 8, 7, and 9.

Subtract 1 from Multiples of 10 (3 minutes)

Materials: (T) Drawings on the board should be sufficient.
              Cover rows and reveal them as the numbers grow.

Note: This fluency sequence assures that students can change
from thirty to twenty-nine, forty to thirty-nine. In Say Ten
counting, it is from "3 tens" to "2 tens 9," "4 tens" to "3 tens 9."
Continue through 100 – 1. You might do the problems in order
at first and then jumble the sequence.

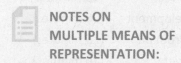

NOTES ON MULTIPLE MEANS OF REPRESENTATION:

Coupled with Say Ten counting, these
representations help students to
understand the unit changes occurring
at the tens. Connect Say Ten language
with models such as the 100-bead
Rekenrek.

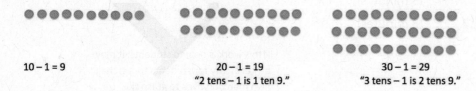

10 – 1 = 9   20 – 1 = 19   30 – 1 = 29
              "2 tens – 1 is 1 ten 9."   "3 tens – 1 is 2 tens 9."

Concept Development (20 minutes)

Materials: (T) Two-color counters and ten-frame cards showing
              10 (S) Personal white boards and markers

Note: The focus in this section is on subtracting single-digit
numbers from multiples of 10 at least through 100 (e.g., 20 – 1;
20 – 5; 30 – 3; 40 – 6; 50 – 1; 50 – 6; 60 – 7; 100 – 8).

T: Present 10 counters (as shown to the right).

T: 10 – 3 is?

S: 7.

T: (Lay down a ten-frame card.) 10 + 7 is?

S: 17.

T: 20 – 3 is?

Lesson 8:   Decompose to subtract from a ten when subtracting within 100 and
              apply to one-step word problems.
Date: 6/25/13

1.C.27

S: 17.

T: 10 + 10 − 3 is?

S: 17.

T: (Lay down a ten-frame card.) 20 + 7 is?

S: 27.

T: 30 − 3 is?

S: 27.

T: 20 + 10 − 3 is?

S: 27.

T: Explain to your partners how 10 − 3 helps us to solve 30 − 3. Use the model to help you.

S: They're the same, but 30 has 2 more tens. → 10 is inside 30 so you take from the ten. → It's the same as 20 + 10 − 3.

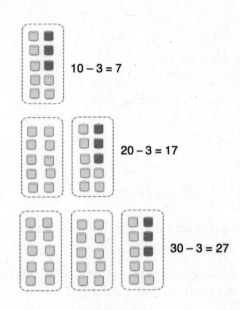

10 − 3 = 7

20 − 3 = 17

30 − 3 = 27

Following the work with manipulatives, model how to draw the number bond in order to solve the problems.

Take the 3 from the ten. Give the students a variety of problems from simple to complex such as those listed above (e.g., 20 − 1, 40 − 1, 70 − 1 or 40 − 7, 80 − 7, 100 − 7). Conclude with a brief discussion about the helpfulness of the structure (MP.7).

T: 90 − 3 = 87. Discuss with your partner how 10 − 3 helps to solve 90 − 3.   Use a drawing or materials that will help you to explain clearly.

T: 60 − 8 can be solved using the same way of thinking. Can you write and solve other problems that can be solved this way, too?

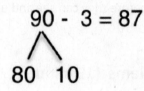

90 - 3 = 87

80   10

Note: In the following activity, the focus is on taking from 10 to subtract (e.g., 31 − 6, 23 − 7, etc.). From prior learning, students know their partners to 10 with automaticity. Therefore this next complexity of adding the ones back after taking from the ten is not too challenging. When students count back to execute this process, it is very hard to see the simplicity of the pattern.

T: Present 11 counters (as shown to the right).

T: 10 − 5 (Pause and point.) + 1 is?

S: 6.

T: 11 − 5 is?

S: 6.

T: (Lay down a ten-frame card.) 20 − 5 is?

S: 15.

T: 21 − 5 is?

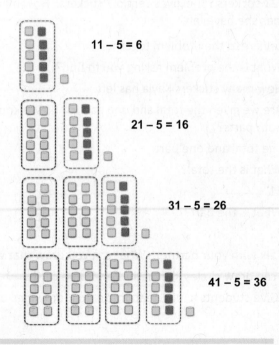

11 − 5 = 6

21 − 5 = 16

31 − 5 = 26

41 − 5 = 36

COMMON CORE™

Lesson 8:   Decompose to subtract from a ten when subtracting within 100 and apply to one-step word problems.

Date: 6/25/13

1.C.28

S: 16.

T: 20 - 5 + 1 is?

S: 16.

T: (Lay down a ten-frame card.) 30 – 5 is?

S: 25.

T: 31 – 5 is?

S: 26.

T: 30 - 5 + 1 is?

S: 26.

T: Explain to your partners how 10 – 5 helps us to solve 21 – 5. Use the model to help you.

S: (Students share.)

As in the previous chunk of the lesson, subtracting from multiples of 10, interactively model for the students how to use the bonds to "get out the 10," subtract the 5 ones from the ten, and add back the remaining part to 81.

T: 91 – 5 = 86. Show your partner how you know that is true. Use your words, number bonds and models to prove it. How might you solve 23 – 9 using the same process?

Note: Allow time for students to work on their personal boards, with manipulatives as needed, so that they practice many problems, challenging those who need greater complexity, going slower for students who need to do more problems before they can see and use the pattern of the basic fact or the structure created by the tens.

Application Problems (15 minutes)

Kayla has 21 stickers. She gives Sergio 7 stickers. How many stickers does she have left?

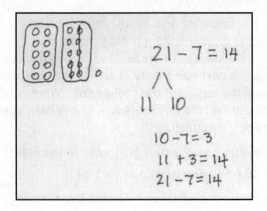

T: Let's read the problem together.

T: What is the problem asking you to find?

S: How many stickers Kayla has left.

T: Are we given the total and one part, or do we know both parts?

S: The total and one part.

T: What is the total?

S: 21.

T: What is the part?

S: 7.

T: Talk with your partner. What can you draw that will help you see the information in the problem?

S: I can draw circles like on the ten-frame cards. → I can draw a number bond.

T: (Give students a minute to make their drawings on their personal boards.)

COMMON CORE™   Lesson 8:   Decompose to subtract from a ten when subtracting within 100 and
                        apply to one-step word problems.   1.C.29
                        Date: 6/25/13

© 2013 Common Core, Inc. All rights reserved. commoncore.org

T: How can I find the difference?

S: Subtract!

T: Can I use the strategy we learned today to solve?

S: Yes! Subtract from the ten.

T: (Circulate as students solve and show their work. Choose one or two pieces of student work to share with the class. Ask the students to share the strategies they used to solve.)

Note: This application problem is an extension of the lesson concept wherein students decompose to subtract from a ten. While the script guides students to use the strategy of subtracting from the ten using ten frames and number bonds, accept all work that students can rationally explain.

Problem Set (10 minutes)

Students should do their personal best to complete the Problem Set within the allotted 10 minutes. For some classes, it may be appropriate to modify the assignment by specifying which problems they work on first. Some problems do not specify a method for solving. Students solve these problems using the RDW approach used for Application Problems.

In this Problem Set, we suggest all students begin with Page 1 and then move on to Problem 4. Possibly leave Problems 2, 3, and 5 to the end if there is still time.

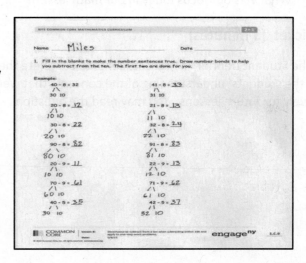

Student Debrief (10 minutes)

Lesson Objective: Decompose to subtract from a ten when subtracting within 100 and apply to one-step word problems.

The Student Debrief is intended to invite reflection and active processing of the total lesson experience.

Invite students to review their solutions for the Problem Set. They should check work by comparing answers with a partner before going over answers as a class. Look for misconceptions or misunderstandings that can be addressed in the Debrief. Guide students in a conversation to debrief the Problem Set and process the lesson. You may choose to use any combination of the questions below to lead the discussion.

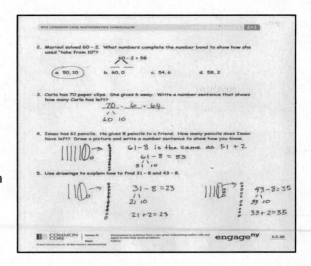

| Lesson 8: | Decompose to subtract from a ten when subtracting within 100 and apply to one-step word problems. | 1.C.30 |
| Date: | 6/25/13 | |

© 2013 Common Core, Inc. All rights reserved. commoncore.org

The following is a suggested list of questions to invite reflection and active processing of the total lesson experience. Use those that resonate for you as you consider what will best support your students' ability to articulate the focus of the lesson.

MP.7

- In the Problem Set, how does 20 – 8 help me

  solve 21 – 8?

- How does 21 – 8 help solve 32 – 8?

  How did the basic fact 10 – 8 = 2 help you to solve 21 – 8 and 32 – 8?

- How do number bonds help you solve subtraction problems?

- What was our focus today in our math lesson?

Exit Ticket (3 minutes)

After the Student Debrief, instruct students to complete the Exit Ticket. A review of their work will help you assess the students' understanding of the concepts that were presented in the lesson today and plan more effectively for future lessons. You may read the questions aloud to the students.

COMMON CORE™

Lesson 8:	Decompose to subtract from a ten when subtracting within 100 and apply to one-step word problems.
Date:	6/25/13

Do as many as you can in 60 seconds.

1	9 and 1 is ___
2	1 more than 9 is ___
3	9 + ___ = 10
4	9 + 1 + 1 = ___
5	10 + 1 =
6	9 + 2 =
7	2 + 9 =
8	9 + 3 =
9	9 + 4 =
10	9 + 1 + 3 =
11	9 + 4 =
12	4 + 9 =
13	9 + 1 =
14	10 + 4 =
15	9 + 4 =

16	9 + 1 =
17	9 + 1 + 2 =
18	9 + 3 =
19	10 + 3 =
20	10 + 4 =
21	10 + 5 =
22	9 + 1 + 5 =
23	9 + 5 =
24	5 + 9 =
25	9 + 6 =
26	10 + 6 =
27	9 + 1 + 6 =
28	9 + 7 =
29	7 + 9 =
30	8 + 9 =

Can you use the ten to make these sums easy?

Robin Ramos 2005

Do as many as you can in 60 seconds.

1	8 and 2 is ___
2	2 more than 8 is ___
3	8 + ___ = 10
4	8 + 2 + 1 = ___
5	10 + 1 =
6	8 + 3 =
7	3 + 8 =
8	8 + 3 =
9	8 + 4 =
10	8 + 2 + 3 =
11	8 + 5 =
12	5 + 8 =
13	8 + 2 =
14	10 + 4 =
15	8 + 4 =

16	8 + 2 =
17	8 + 2 + 2 =
18	8 + 4 =
19	10 + 2 =
20	10 + 3 =
21	10 + 4 =
22	8 + 2 + 4 =
23	8 + 6 =
24	6 + 8 =
25	8 + 6 =
26	10 + 6 =
27	8 + 2 + 6 =
28	8 + 8 =
29	8 + 9 =
30	9 + 8 =

COMMON CORE™   Lesson 8:   Decompose to subtract from a ten when subtracting within 100 and
apply to one-step word problems.
Date: 6/25/13

1.C.32

Name _____   Date _____

1. Fill in the blanks to make the number sentences true. Draw number bonds to help you subtract from the ten. The first two are done for you.

Example:

40 – 8 = 32   41 – 8 = ___

30 10   31 10

20 – 8 = ___   21 – 8 = ___

30 – 8 = ___   32 – 8 = ___

90 – 8 = ___   91 – 8 = ___

20 – 9 = ___   22 – 9 = ___

70 – 9 = ___   71 – 9 = ___

40 – 5 = ___   42 – 5 = ___

COMMON CORE™ | Lesson 8:   Decompose to subtract from a ten when subtracting within 100 and
                   | apply to one-step word problems.
                   | Date: 6/25/13   1.C.33

2. Marisol solved 60 – 2. What numbers complete the number bond to show how she used "take from 10"?

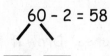

$$60 - 2 = 58$$

_____ _____

    a. 50, 10   b. 60, 0   c. 54, 6   d. 58, 2

3. Carla has 70 paper clips. She gives 6 away. Write a number sentence that shows how many Carla has left?

_____ - _____ = _____

4. Isaac has 61 pencils. He gives 8 pencils to a friend. How many pencils does Isaac have left? Draw a picture and write a number sentence to show how you know.

5. Use drawings to explain how to find 31 – 8 and 43 – 8.

COMMON CORE™

Lesson 8:

Date:

Decompose to subtract from a ten when subtracting within 100 and apply to one-step word problems.

6/25/13

1.C.34

© 2013 Common Core, Inc. All rights reserved. commoncore.org

Name _____   Date _____

Solve the following 4 problems. Show your number bonds. Draw if that will help you.

1. 20 – 8 = _____   2. 60 – 5 = _____

3. 21 – 8 = _____   4. 62 – 5 = _____

Name _____   Date _____

1. Fill in the blanks to make the number sentences true. Draw number bonds to help you subtract from the ten. The first two are done for you.

Example:

40 – 8 = 32   41 – 8 = ___

30 10   31 10

10 – 3 = ___   11 – 3 = ___

20 – 5 = ___   21 – 5 = ___

50 – 7 = ___   52 – 7 = ___

70 – 8 = ___   71 – 8 = ___

40 – 8 = ___   42 – 8 = ___

COMMON CORE   Lesson 8:   Decompose to subtract from a ten when subtracting within 100 and
apply to one-step word problems.
Date: 6/25/13

© 2013 Common Core, Inc. All rights reserved. commoncore.org

1.C.36

60 – 7 = ___   61 – 7 = ___

80 – 9 = ___   82 – 9 = ___

Solve.

2. Mary solved 40 – 6. Which numbers complete the bond to show how she used "take from 10"?

$$40 - 6 = 34$$

___   ___

a. 3, 3   b. 40, 10   c. 30, 6   d. 30, 10

3. Anne finds 41 leaves. She drops 3. Write a number sentence that shows how many are left.

_____ - _____ = _____

4. Dane has 22 cans. His mother took 5 cans. How many cans does Dane have left? Draw a picture and write a number sentence to show how you know.

Name _____   Date _____

1.   a. Write the numbers to make each number sentence true.

$6 + 4 + 2 =$ _____ $+ 2$ $10 + 3 =$ _____ $+ 3 + 3$ $16 =$ ___ $+ 8 + 6$

   b. Label each number sentence true or false.

         $8 + 3 = 10 + 1$ _____

         $7 + 6 = 10 + 4$ _____

         $4 + 8 = 5 + 9$ _____

         $7 + 8 = 9 + 6$ _____

   c. Use drawings, words, or numbers to show why $18 - 3 = 15$ and $10 + 5 = 15$ have the same answer.

2.   Use number bonds to solve.

$38 + 6 =$	$60 - 4 =$

74 + 9 =	53 – 7 =

3.   Trevor's mom gave him 6 stickers to start his collection. He received 85 more for his birthday.

    a.   Use words, pictures, or numbers to show how many stickers Trevor has now.

    b.   James has 95 stickers and gives away 7. How many stickers does James have now?

    c.   Who has more stickers now, James or Trevor?

4. Mr. Garcia checked out 37 library books for his class. The class read some first month and the remaining 19 books the second month.

    a. Use words, pictures, or numbers to find out how many books the class read in the first month of school.

    b. During the third month, Mr. Garcia checked out 29 more books and his class read them all. Use words, pictures, or numbers to show how many library books have been read in all 3 months.

End- Module Assessment Task Standard Addressed	Topics A-C

Represent and solve problems involving addition and subtraction.

2.OA.1   Use addition and subtraction within 100 to solve one-and two-step problems involving situations of adding to, taking from, putting together, taking apart, and comparing with unknowns in all positions, e.g., by using drawings and equations with a symbol for the unknown number to represent the problem. (See Glossary, Table 1.)

Add and subtract within 20.

2.OA.2   Fluently add and subtract within 20 using mental strategies. (See standard 1.OA.6 for a list of mental strategies.) By end of Grade 2, know from memory all sums of two one-digit numbers.

Use place value understanding and properties of operations to add and subtract.

2.NBT.5   Fluently add and subtract within 100 using strategies based on place value, properties of operations, and/or the relationship between addition and subtraction.

Evaluating Student Learning Outcomes

A Progression Toward Mastery is provided to describe steps that illuminate the gradually increasing understandings that students develop *on their way to proficiency.* In this chart, this progress is presented from left (Step 1) to right (Step 4). The learning goal for each student is to achieve Step 4 mastery. These steps are meant to help teachers and students identify and celebrate what the student CAN do now and what they need to work on next.

A Progression Toward Mastery

Assessment Task Item and Standards Addressed	STEP 1 Little evidence of reasoning without a correct answer. (1 Point)	STEP 2 Evidence of some reasoning without a correct answer. (2 Points)	STEP 3 Evidence of some reasoning with a correct answer or evidence of solid reasoning with an incorrect answer. (3 Points)	STEP 4 Evidence of solid reasoning with a correct answer. (4 Points)
1 **2.OA.2** **2.NBT.5**	The student correctly solves 1-3 out of the 8 parts.	The student correctly solves 4-5 out of the 8 parts.	The student correctly solves 6-7 out of the 8 parts.	Student correctly: ▪ Answers 10, 7, and 2 for part a. ▪ Answers "true" for the first and last problems for part b ▪ Answers "false" for the second and third problems for part b ▪ Uses drawings, words, or numbers to explain reasoning for part c
2 **2.OA.2** **2.NBT.5**	The student correctly solves 1-3 out of the 8 parts.	The student correctly solves 4-5 out of the 8 parts.	The student correctly solves 6-7 out of the 8 parts.	Student correctly: ▪ Draws a number bond to decompose 6 as 2 and 4 to solve 38 + 6 = 44 ▪ Draws a number bond to show 60-4 = 56 ▪ Draws a number bond to show 74 + 9 = 83 ▪ Draws a number bond to show 53 – 7 = 46

A Progression Toward Mastery

3 **2.OA.1** **2.NBT.5**	The student correctly solves 1 out of the 4 parts.	The student correctly solves 2 out of the 4 parts.	The student correctly solves 3 out of the 4 parts.	The student correctly: ▪ Uses words, pictures, or numbers to show 85 + 6 = 91 ▪ Answers 88 ▪ Answers Trevor
4 **2.OA.1**	The student correctly solves 1 out of the 4 parts.	The student correctly solves 2 out of the 4 parts.	The student correctly solves 3 out of the 4 parts.	The student correctly: ▪ Used words, pictures, or numbers to show 18 books ▪ Used words, pictures, or numbers to show 66 books

Name _Tracy_   Date _____

1.   a. Write the numbers to make each number sentence true.

$6 + 4 + 2 = \underline{10} + 2$ $10 + 3 = \underline{7} + 3 + 3$ $16 = \underline{2} + 8 + 6$

    b. Label each number sentence true or false.

$8 + 3 = 10 + 1$ __True__

$7 + 6 = 10 + 4$ __False__

$4 + 8 = 5 + 9$ __Flase__

$7 + 8 = 9 + 6$ __True__

    c. Use drawings, words, or numbers to show why $18 - 3 = 15$ and $10 + 5 = 15$ have the same answer.

00000	$+ 00000$
000	
15	15

2.   Use number bonds to solve.

$38 + 6 = 44$	$60 - 4 = 56$
$2\ \ 4$	$50\ \ 10$
$40 + 4$	

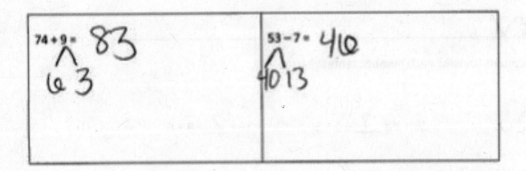

3.   Trevor's mom gave him 6 stickers to start his collection. He received 85 more for his birthday.

a.   Use words, pictures or numbers to show how many stickers Trevor has now.

$$6 + 85 = 91$$

b.   James has 95 stickers and gives away 7. How many stickers does James have now?

$$95 - 7 = 88$$

c.   Who has more stickers now, James or Trevor?

Trevor

4. Mr. Garcia checked out 37 library books for his class. The class read some first month and the remaining 19 books the second month.

    a. Use words, pictures, or number to find out how many books the class read in the first month of school.

$$37 - 19 = 18$$

b. During the third month, Mr. Garcia checked out 29 more books and his class read them all. Use words, pictures, or numbers to show how many library books have been read in all 3 months.

$$37 + 29 = 66$$